EDITOR: LEE JOHNSON

OSPREY MILITARY

ELITE SERIES | **58**

THE JANISSARIES

Text by
DAVID NICOLLE
Colour plates by
CHRISTA HOOK

First published in Great Britain in 1995 by
Osprey, an imprint of Reed Consumer Books Ltd.
Michelin House, 81 Fulham Road,
London SW3 6RB
and Auckland, Melbourne, Singapore and Toronto

© Copyright 1995 Reed International Books Ltd.

All rights reserved. Apart from any fair dealing for the
purpose of private study, research, criticism or review, as
permitted under the Copyright, Designs and Patents
Act, 1988, no part of this publication may be
reproduced, stored in a retrieval system, or transmitted
in any form or by any means, electronic, electrical,
chemical, mechanical, optical, photocopying, recording
or otherwise, without the prior permission of the
copyright owner. Enquiries should be addressed to the
Publishers.

ISBN 1 85532 413 X

Filmset in Great Britain by Keyspools Ltd.
Printed through Bookbuilders Ltd., Hong Kong

If you would like to receive more information about
Osprey Military books, The Osprey Messenger is a regular
newsletter which contains articles, new title information
and special offers. To join free of charge
please write to:

**Osprey Military Messenger,
PO Box 5, Rushden,
Northants NN10 6YX**

Author's dedication
For Dr. 'Paddy' Patricia Baker, in the hope that she
approves.

Author's note
Until 1928 Ottoman Turkish was written in a slightly
modified version of the Persian script, itself a development of the Arabic alphabet. The modern Turkish
alphabet uses standard Latin letters plus a few additional ones with special accents. These, and some of the
standard letters, are pronounced in a way that is unlike
English usage. The most notable differences are the
following:
c – like j in jam; ç – like ch in church; ğ – like y in yet,
or to lengthen preceding vowel; ı – like i in cousin; i –
like i in pit; j – like s in treasure; o – like o in hot; ö –
like German ö in König or French eu in peur; s – like s
in sing; ş like sh in shall; ü – like German ü in Führer
or French u in tu; y – like y in yet.

Publisher's note
Readers may wish to study this title in conjunction with
the following Osprey publications:
MAA 140 *Armies of the Ottoman Turks*
MAA 155 *The Knights of Christ*
MAA 195 *Hungary and the fall of Eastern Europe*
MAA 210 *The Venetian Empire*
MAA 222 *The Age of Tamerlane*
MAA 259 *The Mamluks*

Artist's note
Readers may care to note that the original paintings
from which the colour plates in this book were pre-
pared are available for private sale. All reproduction
copyright whatsoever is retained by the publisher.

All enquiries should be addressed to:
Scorpio Gallery
PO Box 475
Hailsham
E. Sussex BN27 2SL

The publishers regret that they can enter into no
correspondence upon this matter.

THE JANISSARIES

INTRODUCTION

For centuries serious study of the Ottoman Empire and its army has been hampered by prejudice and deep-seated Western fears of the 'Terrible Turk' – fears rooted in centuries of warfare between Christian Europe and its closest Muslim neighbour. Some prejudices run so deep that they are barely visible. For example the traditional costumes of many European circus clowns, their baggy trousers and pointed caps, seem to be a mockery of Ottoman Turkish fashions.

Even today a respected historian can maintain that the Janissaries replaced love of family, home and country with religious frenzy, fanatical obedience, lust for spoils and handsome boys, denying that there was any 'nobility of motive' behind their military successes. In contrast to such silly statements, earlier writers who witnessed the Janissaries in action were far more objective. The early 15th century Greek commentator Chalcondilas put Ottoman success down to strict discipline, an excellent commissariat, maintaining roads in good repair, and having well-ordered camps, large numbers of pack animals and well-organised support services. Writing in the late 16th century, René de Lusinge offered 17 reasons for Ottoman victories; among these were devotion to war, taking the offensive, a lack of interest in fixed fortifications, well-trained soldiers, strong discipline, use of ruses as well as direct attack, good commanders, and no wasting time on amusements. The Austrian ambassador Busbeq added the cleanliness of their camps, where there was neither gambling, drinking nor swearing, and where there were proper latrines and an efficient corps of water-carriers who followed the army into battle and helped the wounded.

Within this impressive force the Janissaries formed one part of the *Kapıkulu* regiments, the Sultan's personal troops recruited from slaves or prisoners. In many ways the Janissaries reflected Ottoman society, which was itself dominated by a military elite and where there was much greater social mobility than in Europe. On top of this, the Turks looked upon Europe much as the early Americans viewed the Western Frontier – as a land of adventure, mission and opportunity.

One characteristic of the Janissary Corps has made it difficult for Westerners to remain objective; the fact that it was recruited from slaves. Yet this should be seen in context. Byzantine and other Balkan Christian armies normally enslaved Muslim or

Ottoman troops at the battle of Çaldıran, 1514, in a manuscript of c.1525. Four infantrymen carry long-bladed and hooked staff weapons. The two in front wear the red Janissary caps of the Silâhtar guard corps, which normally fought as cavalry; the others have the normal white cap of Janissary Cemaat units. Two of these infantrymen also have richly embroidered tunics, perhaps indicating officer status. (Selimname, Ms. Haz. 1597–8, f.113a, Topkapi Lib., Istanbul)

Byzantine infantry on an Italian painted chest of the mid-15th century, showing 'The Ottoman conquest of Trabzon'. Their appearance is different to that in archaic Byzantine art of the period, but is probably an accurate reflection of late Byzantine costume and weaponry. The similarity between their tall hats and those worn by early Ottoman infantry is striking. (Met. Mus. of Art. inv. 1914.14.39 New York)

pagan foes, and the Hospitallers – the epitome of Christian Crusading values – simply killed their Turkish prisoners, while Catalan mercenaries in the area slaughtered all Turks over the age of ten. The Turks, on the other hand, adopted the traditional Muslim practice of not harming POWs under the age of 20, but enslaving them as a booty.

It was, however, against the *Şariat* or Muslim religious law for a ruler to enslave his own Christian subjects. The Ottoman system differed from what had gone before because military slaves were recruited within the state. This *Devşirme* or 'levy of tribute children' provided elite infantry, cavalry and civil servants, evolving during the early years when Ottomans adhered to a strange mixture of unorthodox religious beliefs, Turkish tribal custom and Byzantine tradition. To describe the Janissaries simply as 'slave-soldiers' is misleading. The title of *Kul* or slave was one of pride and dignity, not oppression; even in the 17th century, to be known as a *Kul* was regarded as more honourable than to be a 'subject'.

The early history of the Janissaries is shrouded in myth. The Ottoman state started as one of the smallest Turkish *Beyliks* or principalities in Anatolia at the close of the 13th century, and even though the Ottomans lay closest to the Byzantine heartland, other *Beyliks* took part in the first Turkish penetration of Europe. Indeed, the Ottoman state began as a refuge for soldiers, peasants and townsfolk fleeing the Mongols. Military success attracted more volunteers and in 1362 Murad adopted the title of *Sultan* – his predecessors having been mere *Beys* or *Amirs*. Reconciling the traditions of the *Gazi* warrior class, which soon included the Janissaries, with those of the *Ulema* religious scholars who represented classical Islamic civilization remained a problem for the Ottoman state for many centuries. On top of such divisions, a wave of *Sunni* Muslim orthodoxy swept the Empire in the 16th century, following the Ottoman conquest of the Arab Middle East; and a glance at the map shows that the vast Ottoman Empire remained a collection of almost isolated regions divided by deserts and seas. However, the Ottomans had one great asset: a strong tradition of tolerance, which enabled the Sultan and his Janissaries to control this disparate Empire.

Such tolerance brought immediate rewards, in the form of large-scale conversion to Islam among previously persecuted minorities such as the Bogomils of Bosnia. Many Jews also converted, and were thus able to enter the elite, something they had never been able to do under Christian rule. By giving existing Christian military classes a continuing role while offering the possibility of further advancement if they converted to Islam, the Ottomans absorbed much of the Byzantine Greek and Slav elites, who in turn soon had a clear influence on the development of Ottoman military traditions.

ORIGINS AND EVOLUTION OF THE JANISSARY CORPS

The popular image of conquering Turkish armies as consisting of nomad horse-archers is completely inaccurate where the Ottomans are concerned. Early Ottoman armies were capable of fighting effectively in both mountains and forests, and of conducting combined operations once they had acquired a navy in the mid-14th century. Foot soldiers played a major role throughout, but cavalry remained a dominant arm well into the 18th century.

Ottoman armed forces benefited from an extremely varied military heritage, starting with the Seljuq Turkish rulers of 13th century Anatolia, who had made considerable use of infantry. In fact, after the devastating Mongol invasion, the crumbling Seljuq state increasingly relied on urban *Piyadegan* infantry militias that were often based upon dervish religious associations. Such militias continued into the subsequent era of *Beyliks* or minor principalities. Within these *Beyliks*, religiously motivated groups of *Ahi* volunteers were used to control bandits and to protect travellers. At the same time, increasing numbers of Byzantine *Akritoi* frontier troops were defecting to these little Turkish states. Written sources strongly suggest that the armies of the westernmost *Beyliks* included a majority of infantry, particularly when raiding across the narrow straits to the European mainland. The epic *Düsturname Destan*, relating the adventures of the ruler of the *Beylik* of Aydin, describes his *Azap* infantry archers forming up ahead of his *Gazi* cavalry. For their part, Greek sources refer to Umur's men as *symmachia peze* or 'auxiliary infantry'.

Early Ottoman forces were similar to those of other *Beyliks*, with Christian military elites generally being left in place. Even the new *Yaya* infantry and *Müsellem* cavalry were recruited from both Muslims and Christians, the *Yaya* first appearing in the reign of Orhan (1324–59). As soon as the Ottomans seized control of Thrace in the 1360s, Muslim Turks were settled there to provide readily available foot

Archery equipment. (A–B) 17th century leather quiver of a type normally used on foot. (Askeri Müze, inv. 7553 & 467, Istanbul). (C) 18th century 'log' type of target used in short-range shooting. Comparable targets are shown in 14th century Mamluk manuscripts. (Askeri Müze, Istanbul)

A

B

C

soldiers. Orhan also had a corps of full-time infantry retainers by 1338, but these, like the *Kapıhalkı* bodyguard of the late 14th century, were not yet Janissaries.

Byzantine influence on the development of Ottoman infantry and marines was apparently strong throughout the 14th century. As with the Ottoman the most effective Byzantine troops were, in fact

The Yedikule 'Seven Towers' citadel built against the inside of Istanbul's ancient walls in 1458. It is one of the earliest star-shaped fortifications in Europe. (Author's photograph)

Below: In the 16th–17th centuries, when this anonymous Italian drawing was made, the 'Seven Towers' citadel was full of the garrison's houses, workshops and barracks. Only the mosque's minaret now survives. (Museo Civico Correr, Venice)

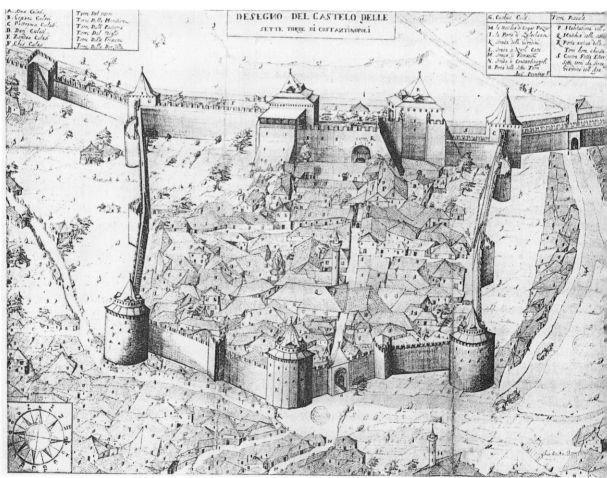

(The Rumeli Hisar, 'Fortress of Europe', on the western shore of the Bosphorus straits. Its great towers, built in 1451–52, were originally covered with conical roofs like those of the Yedikule. Turkish Ministry of Information photograph)

infantry archers. The Byzantine *Mourtatoi* and Serbian *Murtat* were of mixed Christian-Turkish origin or were descended from Turkish prisoners of war, and they included crossbowmen. In contrast, the early 15th century Byzantine *Ianitsarai* were not 'Janissaries', but light cavalry whose name stemmed from the Catalan word *Ginetari* (medieval Latin *Ianizzeri*).

Once established in Europe, the Ottomans also came under Balkan military influence which was itself very varied (the limited available evidence indicates that infantry played a major role in the 14th and 15th centuries); Balkan Christians may even have formed a majority in the full-time Ottoman army during the later 14th century.

It is difficult to separate truth from legend concerning the real origins of the Janissary *Ocak* or Corps. Most traditional accounts credit Orhan with creating the Corps, and almost all give the *Bektaşi* dervish sect a major role, if only in the design of the Janissaries' distinctive *Börk* or white felt cap. One version says that Ali Paşa, Orhan's military adviser, suggested that the ruler's new troops wear white hats to distinguish them from the rest of the army, who wore red (Ali Paşa may actually have been a *Bektaşi* dervish, for the idea was then given religious approval by the sect's leader).

Evidence concerning the origins of the Janissaries may be hidden within this question of distinctive headgear. In earlier centuries, red hats had been worn by revolutionary Shia Muslim groups and may date back to the pre-Islamic *Mazdak* sect. On the other hand, fluffy *zamt* red hats were characteristic of the Sunni Muslim Mamluks in the late 14th century, the military elites of 14th century Christian Byzantium wore red, yellow or black caps, and Christians living under Turkish rule in western Anatolia were characterised by red or white hats. Red hats were worn by most of the Turkish *Beys*, and Orhan may have adopted white to be different. On the other hand tall white *Ak Börk* felt hats may simply have distinguished his slave-recruited troops from those of free origin.

Early Ottoman rulers had probably taken their traditional one-fifth of booty in cash. Large-scale recruitment of prisoners of war began only after the Ottoman conquest of Thrace in the early 1360s. One tradition states that the first such recruits were Byzantine troops captured by Gazi Evrenos, himself of Byzantine origin, following his seizure of Ipsala, south of Edirne. In subsequent years, if the numbers of POWs was insufficient, the Sultan's agents bought fit young slaves in the ordinary slave market to train them as soldiers. Whether these units were inspired by guard units of *Ghulam* slave-recruited cavalry which existed elsewhere in the Middle East is unknown. The first Janissary *Ortas* or battalions were, however, raised to supplement the *Yaya* infantry, and may have been attached to the Sultan's 'hunting establishment'.

The origin or inspiration of the *Devṣirme* system is even less clear: the Byzantine Empire may have forcibly recruited one in five children from some Slav and Albanian areas in the 11th century; Kara Rustem, a mid-14th century Turkish scholar, might have thought up the idea of enlisting captive children as well as adults; or it may have been an original Ottoman idea, or a fusion of new and earlier concepts. Whatever its origin, the *Devṣirme* system clearly emerged after the establishment of the Janissary Corps itself, though it was suspended dur-

ing the chaos that followed Tamerlane's invasion when the Janissaries and other *Kapıkulu* units were virtually wiped out at the battle of Ankara in 1402.

Murat II revived the *Devṣirme* in 1438, upgraded *Kapıkulu* influence and changed the Janissaries' preference for expansion eastwards towards conquests in Europe. The next Ottoman ruler, Mehmed II (1451–81), who conquered Byzantine Constantinople/Istanbul, increased the Janissaries' pay and numbers, gave them improved weaponry, and made them the nucleus of the entire Ottoman army. He also

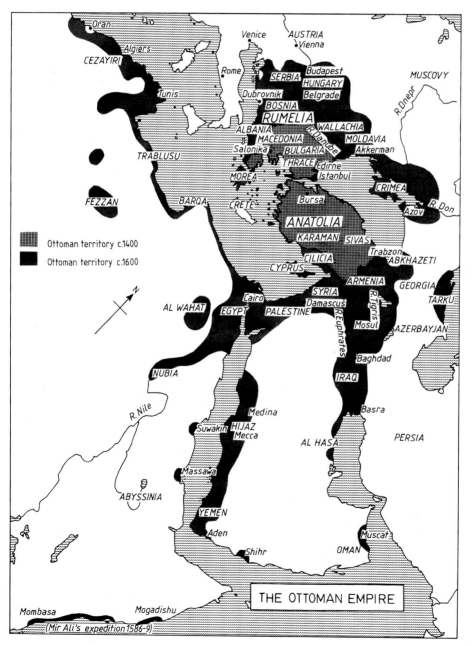

Right: The citadel of Tokat, perched on a rock overlooking the river, has 28 towers. It was constantly strengthened over the centuries, and housed a strategically important garrison while serving as a base for several eastern campaigns. (Author's photograph)

replaced disloyal units with some 7,000 *Sekban* 'dog-handlers' and *Doğancı* 'falconers' from the Royal Hunt in the hope of instilling greater discipline. Some while later the more numerous *Bostancı* 'gardeners' were also converted into fully fledged soldiers to form a third division of the Janissary Corps. Two smaller elites within the *Bostancı* division were the *Hasekis*, who served as the Sultan's infantry guard, and the *Sandalcıs*, who rowed his imperial barge.

There were probably no more than 1,000 Janissaries in the early 14th century, but a detailed estimate of the Ottoman army in 1475 suggests 6,000 Janissaries, 3,000 *Kapıkulu* cavalry, 22,000 *Sipahı* cavalry from the European provinces and 17,000 *Sipahıs* from Anatolia. A specific register for the year 1527 gave Süleyman the Magnificent 87,927 men in his 'Outer Service', of whom 37,627 were *Kapıkulu*, including Janissaries, cavalry and technical troops. Ottoman documents captured after the failed siege of Vienna in 1683 show that the Janissaries constituted one quarter of the invasion force, excluding camp-followers. After further defeats in 1699, the Janissary Corps was reduced, but it soon rose again and by the mid-18th century the Ottoman state maintained no fewer than 113,400 Janissaries, though only a minority were real sol-

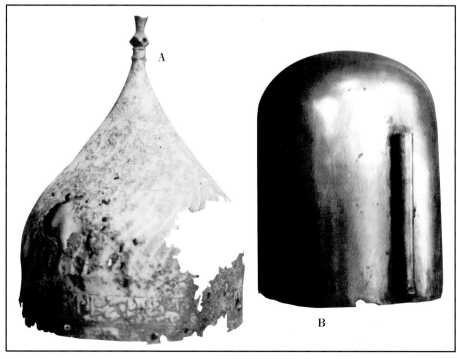

A) The earliest known Ottoman helmet is the so-called 'helmet of Orhan Gazi' who ruled the expanding Ottoman state in the mid-14th century. The inscription is dedicated to Orhan, but the helmet itself could have been worn by one of his commanders or one of his guardsmen. (Askeri Müze, Istanbul). (B) Most surviving Ottoman helmets were for cavalry or were highly decorated objects worn by senior officers. Those dating from the later centuries are generally of copper or brass. This plain brass helmet could have gone beneath a tall Janissary cap and was probably used by an officer. (Askeri Müze, Istanbul)

The Bosnian city of Mostar in happier times. The famous Stari Most 'Old Bridge' was one of the finest pieces of Ottoman architecture in the Balkans until it was recently destroyed by Croatian artillery. Even during the peaceful centuries of Ottoman rule it was a strategic communications link, defended by a tower on the left and garrisoned by locally recruited infantry. (Author's photograph)

Whereas in Europe the state became the master of its armies, the contractual nature of slavery in the Ottoman Empire meant that the Sultan could not dismiss his dependent slaves simply because they were no longer needed. As a result the Ottoman army became the master of the Ottoman state.

Despite the impact Janissaries made on the battlefield, their importance may have been exaggerated, particularly by European observers, who were astonished by the proficiency of the Janissary *Ocak*. In reality, the early phase of Ottoman expansion was largely carried out by local frontier forces, almost without the Sultan's authority, though the ruler's own *Kapıkulu* army did take the lead during the 15th century. The Ottomans also maintained a remarkably sophisticated grasp of grand strategy and 'combined operations', where infantry again played a primary role. On the northern shore of the Black Sea, the Genoese outpost at Kaffa was known as 'the last town in Europe' while less than four hundred kilometres away, Genoese Tana was soon to become known as 'Islam's frontier barrier'. The conquest of these outposts may have turned the Black Sea into an Ottoman lake, but the Turks still took care to 'plug' the huge Black Sea rivers with strong infantry garrisons.

The role of Ottoman naval infantry dates from Orhan's conquest of the Karası *Beylik* and his seizure of its fleet. From then until the late 18th century Janissaries, *Azaps* and *Levents* provided a force of highly effective marines. The long and vulnerable Ottoman coastline would eventually need to be protected against the Portuguese, Dutch, French and British maritime empires by large forces of reliable musket-armed infantry.

RECRUITMENT AND TRAINING

Some Ottoman legal experts tried to justify the *Devşirme* on the grounds that those recruited were not 'protected people' because their ancestors had been conquered by force, or that the Slav and Albanian areas had only converted to Christianity after the Prophet Muhammad's mission in Arabia. But such arguments cut little ice with strict Muslim scholars, who continued to regard the *Devşirme* as gross violation of the rights of the Sultan's non

diers, plus 12,000 *Bostancıs*, 50,000 *Levent* infantry or marines, 3,000 *Mısırlı* auxiliary infantry in Egypt and at least 6,000 other auxiliary foot soldiers.

Early Janissaries, like other Ottoman infantry, were archers, but they soon adopted the arquebus hand-gun (*Arkibuza*) from their Balkan neighbours. Dalmatia, for example, imported guns from Italy as early as 1351, a year before the Ottomans established their first bridgehead on the far side of the Balkan peninsula, and by the early 15th century the *Arkibuza* is mentioned in Bulgarian sources. Ottoman infantry certainly used firearms early in the 15th century, but Murat II was the first ruler to have his men adopt them on a large scale. (The later decline of the Janissaries had nothing to do with any lack of interest in new weaponry, though there was resistance to copying European infantry tactics in the late 17th and 18th centuries.)

Muslim subjects. Not surprisingly, the Orthodox Christian hierarchy was also deeply disturbed by the *Devşirme* – though primarily because it involved conversion to Islam. The Ottomans even claimed that there was no enforced conversion, while maintaining that moral pressure was justified because the Prophet Muhammad had once said: '*All men are born with the seeds of Islam in their hearts.*' Like the far more brutal Spanish Inquisition, those who browbeat young *Devşirme* recruits considered that they were saving souls from hell.

The *Devşirme* was roughly based on the recruiting of one child from every 40 households; this was carried out approximately once every five years somewhere in the Balkans. In its fully developed form the *Devşirme* forcibly enlisted between 1,000 and 3,000 youths in a year, out of a normal total recruitment of up to 8,000 male slaves, until the continuing shortage of military manpower meant that Muslim volunteers were finally allowed into the Janissary Corps late in the 16th century.

The Balkans contributed the largest number of recruits, but the Christian minorities of Anatolia did not escape; the first recorded eastern *Devşirme* was in 1512. On the other hand, many conquered regions had been given immunity from the *Devşirme* in their original surrender terms. Generally speaking, big

Left: One of the earliest reliable illustrations of a Janissary officer's uniform is this drawing by the late 15th century Italian artist Gentile Bellini or by one of his students. (Bellini did visit Istanbul.) This officer is still armed with a bow, whereas many Janissary soldiers were already adopting firearms. His quiver is of a cavalry type. (Inv. 47033/3, British Museum, London)

Above: The castle of Valpovo, in eastern Croatia, stood on the route taken by many Ottoman campaigns and was a vital defensive position against later Hapsburg counter-attacks. Like almost all fortifications in this war-torn region, it dated from much earlier but was strengthened by the Ottomans. (Author's photograph)

cities and off-shore islands were exempt, as were tributary provinces. The *Devşirme* preferred young men aged between eight and 20 from rural peasant families; healthy but uneducated individuals rather than 'street-wise' city youths. Families with only one son were excused, and Jews were exempt. Most Greeks also escaped because the majority of Greek-speakers were then city or island folk. Other exempt groups included miners and those living on strategic roads or passes who already had local defence duties.

Once the shocking novelty of the *Devşirme* wore off, many families volunteered their children for what was seen as a potentially good career, both Christian and Muslim parents reportedly offering bribes so that their children would be accepted. Officially the only Muslims included in the *Devşirme* were the Slav converts of Bosnia. These recruits normally skipped the first stage of training and went directly into an elite *Bostancı* unit.

The *Devşirme* started with a *Ferman* or edict from the Sultan. An officer of at least *Yayabaşı* rank with letters of authorisation and accompanied by several *Sürücü* 'drovers', a secretary and a supply of uniforms, went to a selected area where Christian priests had been made responsible for assembling the male children with their certificates of baptism. Two lists were made of those eligible and fit for service, one was given to a *Sürücü*, who then escorted the recruits to Istanbul. There the most intelligent were sent as *İç Oğlan* or 'inner (service) boys' to the Sultan's Palace Schools, destined, with luck, for high office. The rest, the *Acemi Oğlan* or 'foreign boys', were sent to the households of senior or respected men for the first phase of their education. The selection procedure, supervised by a board of examiners, was a remarkable mixture of archaic and new ideas: on the one hand the strong Turkish belief in the 'science of physiognomy' maintained that moral status could be judged by outer appearance, on the other, the recruits were subject to mental examinations similar to modern IQ tests.

More is known about the education of elite *İç Oğlans* than of ordinary *Acemi Oğlans* destined for the Janissary Corps, yet the principles were similar.

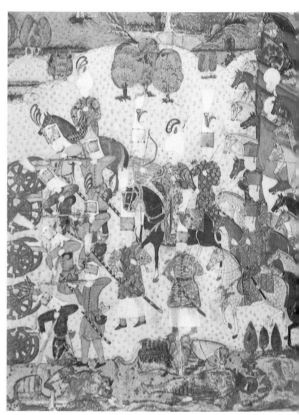

Above: The Devşirme *or 'Recruitment of Tribute Children' in the Süleymanname of 1558. Boys in new red uniforms wait while the* Devşirme Emini, *a senior Janissary officer in charge of recruitment, sorts travel expenses for the boys to go to Istanbul. On the right a Janissary soldier, himself once recruited by the* Devşirme, *reassures an anxious mother and her black-robed priest. (Ms. Haz. 1517, f.31b, Topkapi Lib., Istanbul)*

Right: The battle of Mohács, 1526, in which the Ottomans destroyed the Hungarian army, from the Süleymanname of 1558. Janissary musketeers with a variety of hat-plumes shoot from behind a line of cannon. Behind them stand officers in tall caps, armed with bows. Mounted Silâhtar guardsmen with red Börk Janissary caps are behind these officers. (Ms. Haz. 1517, f.220a, Topkapi Lib., Istanbul)

here were Palace schools at Bursa, Edirne, Istanbul nd Galata, where students studied for two to seven ears under strict discipline imposed by the *Kapı ğası* or 'chief white eunuch'. First they learned bout Islam and were given a general education by *ocas* or 'professors'. Their subsequent line of study epended on what suited them best, be it religious, lministrative or military. Specific subjects included urkish, Persian and Arabic literature, horse-riding, velin-throwing, archery, wrestling, weight-lifting, ıd music for those with a talent. Great emphasis was so put on honesty, loyalty, good manners and self-ontrol. At the end of this training there was a *çıkma*, selection and promotion process. The best *Iç ğlans* went to the Greater or Lesser Chambers of ıe Sultan's Palace, while the rest were transferred to ıe *Kapıkulu* cavalry.

Compared with this almost 'knightly' education, ıat of the ordinary *Acemi Oğlan* was entirely mili-ry, with an overwhelming emphasis on obedience. hey were first hired out as *Türk Oğlan*, to work as rm labourers for Turkish families, to learn Turkish, ısic military skills and the Muslim faith for five to ven years. They were then sent to one of the *Acemi cak* or 'training corps' when vacancies became ailable. Some *Acemi Oğlans* had their initial educa-on in the *Konaks* or households of powerful *Paşas* or *eys*, these being miniature mirrors of the Palace chools. The best of the *Türk Oğlans* were promoted ıto the *Bostancı* or 'gardeners' division instead of ecoming ordinary Janissaries or went to the *Ortas* of ıltacı or 'woodcutters' or to one of the Admiralty *rtas*. From here men were selected for the more chnical *Ortas* of *Cebeci* (armourers), *Topçu* (gun-ers), or *Top Arabacı* (gun-carriage drivers). The ıajority, however, trained in teaching barracks as mple Janissary infantrymen and their classes still ıcluded basic mathematics. The *Acemi Oğlans* also orked in the imperial kitchens or in naval dock-ırds.

Training lasted at least six years, during which me the *Acemi Oğlan* was supervised by eunuchs and ·parated from female company. Discipline was very rict, though the *Acemi Oğlans* were allowed to let off eam in off-duty hours. Final *Kapıya Çıkma* promo-ons into an operational *Orta* were only done when a ıcancy became available, and the passing out parade as a solemn occasion. Graduates marched in single

The siege of Rhodes in 1522, from the Süleymanname of 1558. While Ottoman sappers excavate mines, Janissary marksmen shoot at the Knights Hospitaller

manning the walls. Other Janissaries with shields and hooked pole-arms stand ready to mount an assault. (Ms. Haz. 1517, f.149a, Topkapi Lib., Istanbul)

file, each holding the hem of the man in front, then lined up in front of an *Odabaşı* of their new unit, who gave each the distinctive Janissary hat and a certifi-cate of acceptance. The following evening, after prayers, each new Janissary would put on a soldier's *dolama* or coat and become a full member of the *Ocak*. He would kiss the hand of his new officer who would then address him as a *Yoldaş* or 'travelling companion'. Surprisingly, perhaps, there is clear evi-dence that many Janissaries maintained contact with their original Christian families.

During the period of Ottoman greatness, the ordinary Janissary soldier was trained to use a variety of weapons. Those stationed in Istanbul went to the *Ok Meydan* 'archery ground' just north of the Golden Horn, and practised archery, musketry, jave-lin-throwing or fencing, using old felt hats on poles as fencing targets. Musket shooting was practised against clay pots on the ground or on walls. The men

Above: The fortress of Lipova overlooks a strategic route between eastern Transylvania and Hungary. Under Ottoman rule it was the capital of a Sancak or military district. (Author's photograph)

Right: The fall of Rhodes in 1522, from the Süleymanname of 1558. Some Janissaries shoot at fleeing foes while others seize prisoners or lead them away with ropes around their necks. (Ms. Haz. 1517, f.154b, Topkapi Lib., Istanbul)

shot *'from a great distance'*, according to a French observer, and *'held their guns with one hand'*. The Janissaries' enemies also noted that Ottoman marksmen could shoot accurately by moonlight, while the speed and accuracy of Ottoman musketry still amazed the Austrians in the late 17th century.

In later years recruitment changed completely. In 1568 a select few sons of retired Janissaries were allowed into the Corps, and from 1582 onwards freeborn men were permitted to become 'protégés' of the *Yeniçeri Ağası* or Commander of the Janissaries. The soldiers themselves seem to have favoured phasing out the *Devşirme* so as to open up opportunities for their own sons, and by the end of the 16th century the majority of recruits were probably the sons of Janissaries. In 1594 the ranks were opened to all Muslim volunteers. The *Devşirme* effectively stopped in 1648, though the *Acemi Oğlan* training system remained in place and a final, though unsuccessful, European *Devşirme* was attempted in 1703. By then, the main source of 'human booty' was via the Crimean Tatars of the Ukraine and southern Russia, but even that ended with the Russian annexation of the Crimea in 1783.

OTTOMAN ARMY STRUCTURE – INFANTRY FORCES

During the 15th, 16th and 17th centuries the *Seyifi* or complete military structure of the Ottoman Empire consisted of the Navy, the *Eyâlet Askerleri* 'Provincial Forces' and the *Kapıkulu Askerleri* Sultan's Army. The Navy included naval warfare 'specialists' and *Levents* or marines, while the *Eyâlet Askerleri* and *Kapıkulu Askerleri* each had infantry and cavalry divisions. *Eyâlet Askerleri* provincial infantry were known as *Yerlikulu Piyâdesi* or 'local infantry'. It consisted of the *Müsellem* or 'recognised' troops who, though originally cavalry, had been downgraded to little more than an infantry militia. Then there were the *Icâreli* or 'mercenaries', the *Azaps* and the non-naval *Levents*. Provincial *Sekban* reappeared as provincial infantry in the later period but must not be confused with earlier elite *Sekbans* he Janissary *Ocak*. *Lağımcı* ('sappers' or 'pioneers') were also included in the provincial infantry.

Infantry of the *Kapıkulu Askerleri* or Sultan's Army were known as *Kapıkulu Piyadesi* and included the entire Janissary *Ocak* or Corps. In addition there were *Acemi Oğlan* or training units, the *Cebeci* or corps of armourers, the *Saka* or water-carriers, and *Topçu* or artillery, the *Toparabacı* or gun-carriage corps and the *Humbaracı* or grenadiers, these latter three being regarded as part of the artillery.

The 34 *Acemi Oğlan* training units were the most ancient *Ortas* and, being separate from the rest of the Janissary *Ocak*, were split between two *Meydans* or training centres. The active-service *Ocak* consisted of three sections: the largest, called the *Cemaat* or 'assembly'; the *Bölük* or 'division'; and the *Seğmen* or 'dog handlers'. Within the *Cemaat*, the *Solak Ortas* formed an elite guard (first mentioned in 1402). They remained as infantry archers for many centuries and, like other guard units, were small formations. The *Mütefferikas*, sons of high officials and vassals, appear to have been included among the Solaks. The *Seğmen* were perhaps a less personal guard armed with matchlock guns and short swords. Their units also seem to have been small, of between 50 and 70 men.

The *Bostancı* corps of 'gardeners' was essentially separate from the ordinary Janissaries, primarily be-

ing responsible for the maintenance, policing and defence of some 70 imperial estates as well as the coasts around Istanbul. The associated *Haseki* infantry guard was in charge of all cannon within Palace grounds.

All divisions of the Janissary *Ocak* drew recruits from the *Acemi Oğlan* training *Ortas*, and each *Orta* had the same basic internal structure. This reflected the fact that *Ortas* were at first very small – around 50 men in the mid-15th century rising to 100 in the 16th – and the command structure also reflected the original need to feed slaves who depended on the Sultan. Basically it consisted of the *Orta*'s commanding officer, called a *Çorbasi* or 'soup man', supported by six officers and a larger number of NCOs plus an administrative clerk and an *Imam* or chaplain. Of these only the *Çorbasi* was appointed from outside the unit. *Acemi Oğlan* trainee *Ortas* were also commanded by *Çorbasis* whereas *Solak Ortas* were led by higher ranking *Solakbaşıs* assisted by two other officers.

The Sultan selected the *Yeniçeri Ağası* or Commander of Janissary Corps; the latter usually came

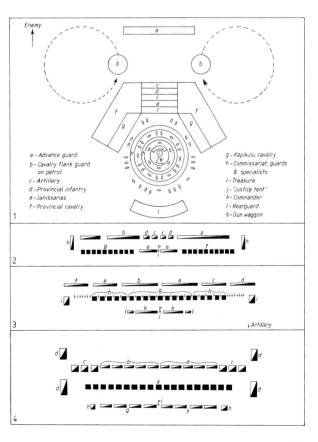

: Schematic layout of Ottoman army encampment at Brandkirken in 1683, based on a plan in Marsigli, l'Etat Militaire de Empire Ottoman.

: Ottoman array at the Battle of Sivas, 1473 (after Von Pawlikowski-Cholewa). (A) European Timar cavalry. (B) Asian Timar cavalry. (C) Gurebâ Kapikullu cavalry. (D) Mercenary cavalry. (E) Sipahi cavalry. (F) Janissaries. (G) Azap infantry. (H) Akıncı cavalry. (I) Commander.

: Ottoman array at the Battle of Marj Dabiq, 1516 after Von Pawlikowski-Cholewa). (A) Asian Timar cavalry. (B) European

Timar cavalry. (C) Cavalry levy from Karaman. (D) Gurebâ Kapikullu cavalry. (E) Cavalry levy from Amasya. (F) Kurdish vassal cavalry. (G) Janissaries. (H) Azap infantry. (I) Akıncı cavalry. (J) Commander. (K) Sipahi cavalry. (L) Mercenary cavalry.

4: Standard Ottoman array of the late 16th century (after Von Pawlikowski-Cholewa). (A) Asian Timar cavalry. (B) European Timar cavalry. (C) Gurebâ Kapikullu cavalry. (D) Akıncı cavalry. (E) Janissaries. (F) Sipahi cavalry. (G) Silâhtar guard cavalry. (H) Flank cavalry units. (I) Commander.

a - Advance guard
b - Cavalry flank guard on patrol
c - Artillery
d - Provincial infantry
e - Janissaries
f - Provincial cavalry

g - Kapikulu cavalry
h - Commissariat, guards & specialists
i - Treasure
j - "Justice tent"
k - Commander
l - Rearguard
◊ - Gun waggon

Enemy

↓ Artillery

from the Corps, having earlier been trained in one of the Palace Schools. The *Yeniçeri Ağası* was a very powerful figure, and even the Grand Vezir could not give him orders directly: all instructions had to go via the Sultan. On the other hand the *Yeniçeri Ağası* had to consult the Janissary Corps' *Divan* or Council in his dealings with the *Ocak*. The Council consisted of the *Yeniçeri Ağası* himself, the *Kul Kâhyası* and *Sekbanbaşı* commanding the *Bostancı* and *Sekban* units respectively, and the COs of three elite 'hunting' *Ortas* (the *Zağarcıbaşı*, the *Samsuncıbaşı* and the *Turnacıbaşı*). The *Başçavuş* provost of the Janissary *Ocak* also seems to have attended the Council.

The final structure of the Janissary *Ocak* consisted of 196 *Orta* battalions: 101 of *Cemaat*, 61 (or 62) of *Bölük*, and 34 (or 33) of *Sekban*. Many Janissary *Ortas* were also distinguished by their (unusual) origins, or by special names, particular duties or commanding officers who had other functions. The most significant were:

Janissary unit insignia, often used in the form of tattoos. Numbers 1 to 101 are those of Cemaat units; *numbers 2B to 58B are those of Bölük units. The insignia of several units have not been preserved.*

Cemaat division

1st: commanded by the *Kul Kâhyası*, who also commanded *Bostancı* units (the Sultan was registered as a soldier in the 1st *Orta*); it was called a *Deveci* or 'camel drivers' unit because it originally escorted the baggage train.

2nd: a *Deveci*.

3rd: a *Deveci*.

4th: a *Deveci*.

14th: known as *Hasekis* or 'guards', perhaps because Palace *Haseki* units were recruited from it.

17th: known as *Çergecis* or 'ceremonial tent pitchers' because their special tent was placed opposite that of the Sultan while on campaign.

28th: known as *Okçus* or 'archers'.

35th: known as *Sekban Avcısıs* or 'dog keepers' though this was not a *Sekban Orta*.

60th: a *Solak* or imperial guard unit.

61st: a *Solak*.

62nd: a *Solak*.

63rd: a *Solak*.

64th: known as *Zağarcıs* or 'greyhound keepers' originally part of the Sultan's hunting establishment; one of two lance-armed cavalry *Ortas*.

65th: originally part of the Sultan's hunting establishment; one of two lance-armed cavalry *Ortas* suppressed by Murad IV for involvement in murder of Osman II.

71st: known as *Samsuncus* or 'mastif keepers'; originally part of the Sultan's hunting establishment

73rd: known as *Turnacıs* or 'crane (bird) keepers' originally part of the Sultan's hunting establishment.

94th: commanded by the chief *Imam* or 'chaplain' of the *Ortas* based in Istanbul.

99th: commanded by the *Şeyh* or leader of the *Bektaşi* dervishes.

101st: commanded by the *Beytülmalci* or chief treasurer of the Janissary Corps.

Bölük division

5th: commanded by the *Başçavuş* or 'provost of the Janissary Corps'.

19th: known as *Bekçi* or sentinels, forming armed guards on campaign.

28th: commanded by the *Muhzır Ağa* or 'summoner' of the Janissary Corps; *Yeniçeri Ağası*'s guard also recruited from it.

The only known complete example of a Aşçı Ustası middle ranking Janissary officer's leather and embossed brass uniform.

It probably dates from the late 18th or early 19th century and is based on a cook's costume. (Askeri Müze, Istanbul)

2nd (or 33rd): commanded by the *Kâhya Yerı* or 'deputy *Kâhya*'.

4th: commanded by the *Talimhaneci* or 'director of the training house'.

5th: permanently stationed as police around Golden Horn; supplying men for the 60-strong *Harbacı* Palace Gate guards who guarded tents of the *Yeniçeri Ağası* and Grand Vezir.

ekban division

8th: also known as *Kâtibis* or 'secretaries', possibly because they served as clerks before *Sekbans* were made a part of the Janissary *Ocak*.

9th: also known as *Kâhyası Sekbanen Ortası* (*Kâhya*'s *Sekban Orta*).

33rd: commanded by the *Avcubaşı*, also known as *Avcıs* or 'huntsmen'; based near the Black Sea in summer, possibly to guard the entrance to the Bosphorus.

The hierarchy of officer ranks in the Janissary Corps might look top-heavy to modern eyes, and may reflect the influence of *Ahi, Fityan* or other Dervish religious brotherhoods during the *Ocak*'s formative years. All 196 *Ortas* were under the *Yeniçeri Ağası*, commander of the Janissary *Ocak* or Corps, but he was only allowed to command the *Ocak* if the Sultan was present. Otherwise the *Yeniçeri Ağası* acted as deputy to whomever the Sultan appointed as Army Commander.

The siege of Rhodes in 1522, from the Süleymanname of 1558. Janissary marksmen shoot at defenders who are inaccurately shown in Turkish-style armour. Other Ottoman troops start to dig trenches while Sultan Süleyman approaches, surrounded by Janissary officers and guardsmen. (Ms. Haz. 1517, f.149b, Topkapi Lib., Istanbul)

Devşirme recruitment in Europe; the *Anadolu Ağas* who supervised 17 training *Ortas* and *Devşirme* recruitment in Asia; and the *Gelibolu Ağası*, who supervised the training of *Ortas* in Gallipoli. As the pattern of Janissary recruitment changed, a new senior rank the *Kuloğlu Başçavuşu*, took charge of training sons Janissaries admitted to the *Ocak*.

The command structure of the *Ortas* also reflected Turkish nomadic tradition, where a tribal leader had been responsible for providing his men with their one meal of the day. Just as the Sultan was known by his Janissaries as 'the father who feeds us the names of *Orta* ranks had a very 'culinary' flavour. It started with the *Çorbacı* 'soup maker' or colonel who was assisted by the *Aşçı Usta* or 'master cook' in charge of one or more *Aşçı* or 'cook' NCOs and the *Baş Karakullukçu* or 'head scullion' junior officer. The rank of *Çavuş* or 'messenger' was roughly equivalent to that of a sergeant, and was also known as a *Karakullukçu* or 'scullion'. The only *Orta* officer with a solely military title was the *Bayraktar* or standard-bearer. Other officers dealing with the *Orta*'s material and spiritual welfare included the *Odabaşı* or 'barrack-room chief', the *Vekilharç* or quartermaster, the *Sakabaşı* or 'head of water distribution', and the *Imam* or 'prayer leader'.

The relative status of these officers is not clear but probably went from the *Sakabaşı* at the bottom up through the *Baş Karakullukçu*, *Aşçı Usta*, *Imam Bayraktar*, *Vekilharç*, *Odabaşı* to the *Çorbacı* at the top. The ordinary *Nefer* or *Yoldaş* soldier was placed in one of three grades according to seniority, starting with the *Eşkinci* or 'campaigner' at the bottom and going to the *Amelimanda* or 'veteran' selected for their proven valour, and to the *Oturak* ('sitter') pensioner, who was not normally required to go on campaign. This highest grade was also permitted to enter a trade.

By the 17th century the most important provincial garrisons were Baghdad, Basra, Damascus, Jerusalem, Aleppo, Cairo, Erzerum, Konya, Van, Khani Corinth, Thessaloniki, Belgrade, Sarajevo, Vidi Budapest, Braîla, Bender, Kaffa, Oczakow an Kaminiec. Most were under the command of Serhad Ağası frontier Ağas, though the larg Janissary garrisons in North Africa formed a virtually independent *Ocak*, that in Algiers even having own *Divan* Council. Elsewhere provincial Janissa

Other senior or 'general staff' officers included: the *Sekbanbaşı* and the *Kul Kâhyası*, both serving as adjutants to the *Yeniçeri Ağas*; the *Istanbul Ağası* in charge of *Acemi Oğlan* trainees and garrison units in Istanbul; the *Ocak Imamı* or 'chief chaplain'; the *Solakbaşı*, who was invariably promoted from the Janissary ranks; the *Beytülmalci* or chief treasurer of the Janissary Corps; the *Muhzır Ağa* or 'summoner' of the Janissary Corps; the *Kâhya Yeri*, who represented the *Yeniçeri Ağası* on the Sultan's Great Council; the *Talimhanecibaşı* in charge of training and military exercises; and the *Azar Başı* or chief of prisons and executions. The *Yeniçeri Kâtibi* or 'secretary' of the Janissary Corps was a civil servant appointed annually to oversee a large staff of bureaucrats, whereas the *Yayabaşı*, originally the commander of *Yaya* infantry but later responsible for Janissary muster rolls, was a soldier. Senior training and recruitment officers included: the *Rumeli Ağası*, who supervised 14 of the training *Ortas* as well as

ructures became increasingly autonomous in the
7th and 18th centuries. In Damascus, for example,
ere were soon two distinct forms of Janissary
oops: the governor's own 'private army' of largely
ssimilated *kapı halkı*, and two *Ortas* of new 'im-
erial' Janissaries sent to take control of the vital
itadel and city gates.

The Janissary *Ocak* also developed its own sys-
m of flags and symbols, but here the Janissaries
ere very different to their European opponents.
he main Janissary *Bayrak* or banner, called the
nam Âzam was of white silk with the inscription:
*Ve give you victory and a sparkling victory. It is God
ho helps us and His help is effective. Oh Muhammad,
ou have brought joyful news to True Believers.*' Tradi-
on states that Orhan gave the first Janissary units a
ed banner with a single white crescent, and that the
hite star which completes the modern Turkish
ational flag was added only after the conquest of
onstantinople/Istanbul. Other motifs on Ottoman
anners included a sun, stars, a dagger, geometric
napes, the 'Hand of Fatima' and *Dhu'l Faqar*, the
ouble-bladed 'Sword of Ali'. Even more distinctive
as the *Tuğ* or Turkish horsetail banner, whose
tendants marched one day ahead of the main
my.

The most famous and unusual of Janissary sym-
ls was, however, the *Kazan*, a large copper cooking
ot that was each *Orta*'s most treasured possession.
he men's ration of *pilav* – boiled *bulgar* (cracked
heat) and butter – was cooked in the *Kazan*, and
ey assembled around it for their one meal of the
ay. When the *Kazan* was carried on parade, every
oldier and officer stood in respectful silence. To tip
ver the *Kazan* was a sign of mutiny, and to take
fuge next to it was to find sanctuary. In battle, an
rta's *Kazan* served as a rallying point in case of
ifficulty, but if the *Kazan* was lost, the defending
fficers were disgraced and the entire *Orta* lost its
ght to parade with other *Kazans*.

Ottoman standards and banners. (A–B) Horse-hair tuğ with boars' teeth crests (Arsenal Museum, Vienna). (C) Horse-hair tuğ, late 17th century (Badisches Landesmuseum, Karlsruhe). (D) Gilded standard-finial (Askeri Müze, Istanbul). (E) Early Ottoman bronze standard-finial (Topkapi Museum, Istanbul). (F) Unit flag (Arsenal Museum, Vienna). (G) Early 18th century Janissary unit flag (after Marsigli). (H) Unit banner (Rathaus Museum, Vienna). (I) Late 17th century battle standard (after Teatro della guerra contro il Turco, Venice 1687). (J) Sancak provincial flag (private collection). (K) Ottoman battle standard cut down in size at a later date (Badisches Landesmuseum, Karlsruhe). (L) Simplified view of commander's flag (after Marsigli).

side one of the firing lleries of the Karababa rtress overlooking the arrow straits between voia and the Greek ainland. This powerful stle was built in 1686, *when the Venetians, holding the nearby island of Tenos as a naval base, still threatened the heart of the Ottoman Empire. (Author's photograph)*

The Tower of the Adâlet Pavilion, almost all that remains of the once magnificent Sarayiçi palace outside Edirne. It was built in 1561 as a symbolic rather than real fortification. Janissaries who distinguished themselves in battle could hope for a transfer to one of the elite units guarding such palaces. (Author's photograph)

UNIFORMS AND WEAPONRY

Ottoman costume was based on Persian rather than Arab tradition and remained remarkably unchanged from the 15th to the early 19th century. Each social class and ethnic, religious, civil or military group had a distinctive way of dressing. Headgear was particularly important in denoting rank. An observant early 15th century Western visitor, the Burgundian squire Bertrandon de la Broquière, described early Ottoman costume as consisting of: '. . . *two or three thin, ankle-length cotton robes one over the other. For a coat they wear a felt robe called a capinat (Turk: Kapaniçe). It is light and very water-proof . . . They wear knee-high boots and wide breeches . . . into which they stuff all their robes so that they will not get in the way when they are fighting or travelling or busy.*'

The uniforms of Janissary soldiers were largely wool, the cloth being made by Jewish weavers in Thessaloniki. The *Börk* and *Üsküf* hats were, however, their most distinctive features and these again reflected dervish influence on the Corps' origins. A simple wooden spoon was attached to the front of this cap as a badge, in yet another example of how the Janissary *Ocak* used culinary symbolism. Senior officers' jackets were edged with fur; fox, squirrel,

ermine, sable, lynx and marten were preferred Janissary boots were red leather, except those o senior officers and privileged units, which were ye low. Belts and sashes also indicated status: those o the nine *Bostancı* ranks were of rough cloth for th lowest grades (1st blue, 2nd white, 3rd yellow, 4t mixed blue and white), fine white cloth for the 5t white silk for the 6th, fine black cloth for the 7th, an black for both 8th and 9th.

Ottoman troops re-used captured weaponry an the Empire also imported large amounts of equip ment from Europe. The Pope's efforts to stop th trade failed, even where Catholic Italy was con cerned, though the main suppliers of military equip ment to the 16th–17th century Ottoman Empir were the Protestant English and Dutch. (An Englis ship seized by the Venetians in 1605 contained n fewer than 700 barrels of gunpowder, 1,000 arquebu barrels, 500 complete arquebuses, 2,000 sword blade and other war materials for the Ottoman army.)

Sales in the opposite direction were on a smalle scale, but in Europe there was demand for high quality Turkish gun-barrels. Arms manufacture wa carried out by distinct guilds that made sword spears, daggers, muskets, pistols and shields, whil heavier weapons were made in state arsenals. strong European influence is, in fact, evident in bot the names and the designs of Ottoman firearms b the 18th century; for example the *müşkat tüfenkleri* o 'flintlock' musket, *karabina* or 'carbine', *tabanca* o 'pistol' and the *çift tabancalı tüfenk* or 'double-barre led pistol'.

Some Janissaries wore full armour during th early days, and siege-assault squads continued to d so for some centuries. But by the 15th centur Ottoman cavalry protection was quite distinct fror infantry protection; most armours popularly labelle 'Janissary' are really *Sipahi* or cavalry armours. Th Janissaries were not issued with heavy weapons i peacetime. Instead these weapons were stored i *Cebehane* or arsenals; the men selected whatever the preferred at the start of a campaign.

At first only a minority of Ottoman infantry ha swords, most only having bows and short spear Most swords and daggers were within long-estab lished Islamic traditions, though pictorial source and surviving weapons suggest a Balkan influence o some. For example, a rare form of broad non-tape g sword with short quillons and a 'mushroom-shaped' pommel has been tentatively identified as Byzantine.

The most common Ottoman sabre was the *kılıç* – broad, non-tapering, and less curved than the slender *cemi kılıç* or Persian sabre. The *gaddara* was a broad, straight or slightly curved 'bowie-knife' of Persian origin, but the origins of the famous reverse or double-curved Turkish *yatağan* and the associated single-edged straight *pala* are still debated. The *meç* was a slender thrusting sword or rapier of Western inspiration, only used by naval troops and by those stationed in Hungary. Assorted maces, such as the *şirz*, *şeşper* and *koçbaşı* or 'ram's head' as well as the *teber* axe were also popular. In addition, Ottoman infantry used various pole-arms (a fact rarely noted by historians). These included the *harba* or guisarme, the *tırpan* or glaive, with a long curved blade, the apparently 'hooked' *zıpkın* and the *balta* or halberd. Some betray Italian influence, presumably from Genoese or Venetian colonies overrun by the Ottomans, but surviving Ottoman pole-arms show equal similarity with Russian weapons, and the *bardiche*, with its tall blade fixed to the haft at two points and large spike at the back, is remarkably similar to Chinese and Central Asian weapons.

Early Janissary *Ortas* consisted of infantry archers, and although most Janissaries were soon armed with guns, the bow remained a prestigious ceremonial weapon throughout the *Ocak*'s history. (Ottoman use of crossbows is less well known, though late Byzantine forces employed them extensively. In fact a late medieval Turkish word for a crossbow, *çanra*, probably came from the Byzantine *tzaggra* – unless both derived from the Persian-Arabic word for crossbow, *jarkh*. Yet it was the Janissaries' use of firearms that caught their enemies' attention. At first the soldiers, proud of their neat appearance, disliked dirty guns, but after witnessing their power in Hun-

(A–B) Front and rear of a Turkish zırh gömlek mail-and-plate cuirass, 16th century. Such armours were worn by Ottoman assault infantry but were more typical of cavalry (Met. Museum, New York). (C) Ottoman Turkish infantry full armour with zırh külâh helmet, 15th century (Met. Museum, New York). (D) Kolluk vambrace, 17th–18th centuries used by assault infantry but more typical of cavalry (Met. Museum, New York). (E) Ottoman shoulder and neck defence, 16th–17th centuries (Met. Museum, New York). (F) Kincal dagger from the Caucasus. (G) Şimşîr Turkish sabre. (H) Yatağan Turkish reverse-curved sword. (I) Ottoman matchlock smooth-bore musket. (J) Rifled flintlock musket from Caucasus. (K) Turkish rifled flintlock musket. (L) Turkish flintlock pistol. (M) flintlock blunderbuss from Albania. (N) Priming flask from Caucasus. (O) Kurdish powder-horn. (P) Turkish powder-horn. (Q) War-axe from Herzegovina. (R) Turkish ceremonial balta halbard. (S) Turkish tırpan staff-weapon. (T) Janissary nacak war-axe. (U) Turkish bıçak dagger. (V) Dagger from Albania.

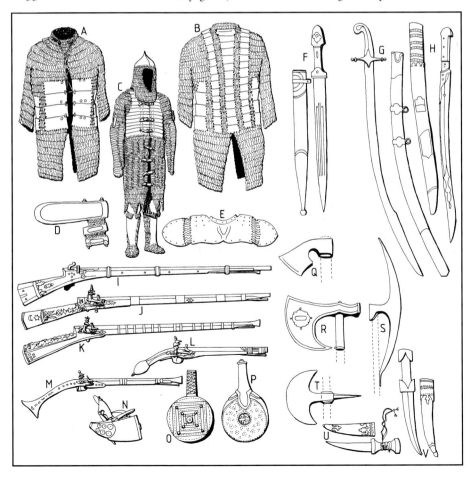

21

gary in 1440–43 the Janissaries gradually accepted the matchlock arquebus.

During these early years guns were known as *tüfenk*, *tüfek* or *zabtanah*, all of which came from medieval Persian words for a blowpipe. Typical Ottoman matchlocks were longer and had a larger bore than those of the West; the largest, from Algiers, could shoot a massive, 80 gm bullet, the lightest, from Greece, a 22 gm bullet. The flintlock system had probably been invented in Germany early in the 16th century, but it remained unreliable in dusty Near Eastern and Middle Eastern conditions. Consequently Ottoman infantry clung to their sturdy matchlocks longer than the rest of Europe. Then, during the 17th century, a simple easy-to-clean flintlock system known as the *miquelet* or 'snaplock' was introduced from Italy or Spain via North Africa.

Not until after the difficult conquest of Venetian Crete in 1645–69 did the Janissaries finally make much use of pistols. In 1770 Baron de Tott, a Frenchman of Hungarian origin, was invited to modernise the Ottoman army, and he tried to get the Turks to use bayonets. But, like the pike before it, this weapon was anathema to the individualistic *Yoldaş*, who realised that it could only be effective if wielded by men acting in unison – or, as the Janissaries saw it, 'fighting like robots rather than warriors'.

STRATEGY AND TACTICS

The Ottoman state was born in the mountains of north-western Anatolia, where warfare consisted of raiding the rich Byzantine valleys and coastal plain or blockading Greek-speaking towns into surrender. Though Turkish tribal cavalry took a leading role in such campaigns, infantry were needed to hold fortified places. The earliest Ottoman campaigns in Thrace, on the European side of the Dardanelles, involved more infantry, and the next phase of expansion, which included the seizure of main roads and mountain passes, again required foot soldiers.

The fast-expanding Ottoman Empire developed a remarkable system of planning, mobilisation and strategic mobility: campaigns were planned well ahead in October and November, with actual operations normally taking place in August and September of the following year. Military leaders consulted old soldiers and the records of previous operations. Huge quantities of stores were sent ahead, before or during mobilisation. Although the Janissaries had reserve supplies of hard biscuit called *peksimet*, they usually ate fresh bread on campaign, as well as *pilav*, onions and fresh mutton or dried beef.

Mobilisation orders went out to provincial forces in December, and it became traditional for an army marching into Europe to assemble near the Davut

Siege-scene from the Süleymanname of 1558. Cannons fire from behind wooden bulwarks filled with earth, and Janissaries man the front-line *trenches while Turkish cavalry drive back an unsuccessful Christian sortie. (Ms. Haz. 1517, Topkapi Lib., Istanbul)*

Paşa mosque in Istanbul, and for those on an Asian campaign to gather at Üsküdar on the eastern side of the Bosphorus. Other troops, from Rumelia, congregated at Thessaloniki, Plovdiv, Sofia, Nis, Eszék in Croatia, Budapest or Timişoara while allied Tatars would gather in Perekop, at the entrance to the Crimean peninsula. The main campaigning centres changed as the Empire expanded, but the most important were: Skopje for the southern Balkan; Thessaloniki for Albania and Greece; Belgrade for Hungary; Kiliya, Izmail, Tulcea, Braila, Silistra and

The fortress at Çeşme on the Aegean coast of Turkey was originally built by the Genoese, probably in the 14th century, but was later strengthened by the Ottomans who also added a mosque and a han or fortified hostel for merchants. (Author's photograph)

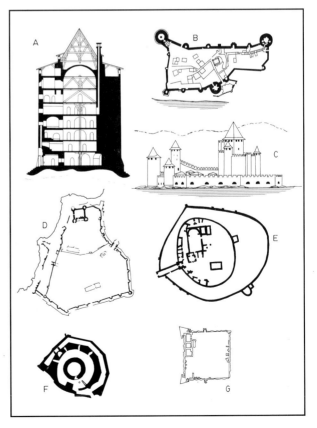

Ottoman fortifications: (A) Section through the main waterfront tower of Rumeli Hisar on the European shore of the Bosphorus, 1452; roof and floors reconstructed (after Gabriel). (B) Plan of Rumeli Hisar, 1452 (after Michell). (C) Reconstruction of Anadolu Hisar on the Asian shore of the Bosphorus, 1395 (after Gabriel). (D) Plan of the fortress at Bilgorod Dnistrovskiy (Turkish: Ak Kirman. Rumanian: Cetatea Alba). The rectangular keep was built in the 14th–15th centuries by the Genoese or Moldavians; the outer walls were strengthened by the Moldavians and Ottomans in the 15th–17th centuries (afer Ionescu). (E) Plan of the castle of Cîlnic in Transylvania. The inner keep dates from the 13th–14th centuries; the outer wall from the Ottoman 16th century (after Anghel). (F) Plan of the castle of Turnu Magulele in Wallachia consisting of a circular 14th century concentric keep, strengthened and with a third wall added in the Ottoman 16th century (after Anghel). (G) Plan of the citadel of Alba Iulia in Transylvania showing the late Ottoman fortifications (after anonymous late 17th century Italian map).

▲ A B ▼

Ottoman and Christian armies face each other across a river in central Europe, from the Süleymanname of 1558. Janissary infantry are concentrated behind guns in the centre, with cavalry on both flanks in a correct, though simplified, representation of typical Ottoman tactics. (Ms. Haz. 1517, Topkapi Lib., Istanbul)

(A) Brass pen-case as used by Janissary Enderunlu and other clerks. It consists of a long container for pens with a sealed inkpot on the side. (Askeri Müze, Istanbul). (B) Detail of a brass belt as used by Janissary junior officers.

The two clasps would have been linked by a thong rather than a piece of wire, as shown here. Such belts came with a great variety of decorative patterns, reflecting the owner's tastes. (Askeri Müze, Istanbul)

Ruse for Wallachia and Transylvania; Bendery, Iaşi, Kaminiec and Khotin for Moldavia; Belgorod for the Dnestr river area; Oczakow and Kilburun for the Dnepr and Bug river areas; Erzerum for Persia; and Diyarbakir, Van and Mosul for Iraq.

Elaborate preparations were made at the start of each campaign, and either the Sultan's six-horsetail banner or the Vezir's three-horsetail banner would be erected in the first courtyard of the Topkapı Palace before being sent ahead to warn of the army's approach. Roads and bridges were repaired along the line of march, with prefabricated pontoon bridges being floated across large rivers. Cairns of stones would be piled up to indicate the way if there were no roads. The most famous military bridge was a forti-

fied wooden structure 6,000 yards long across the marshes and River Drava near Osijek. In the 18th century main roads had a narrow paved strip down the centre for pedestrians and wheeled traffic, with wider strips of cleared and beaten earth on either side for horsemen – much like the ancient Roman roads. The Turks also made great use of four-wheeled waggons, particularly in the Balkans and the grassy steppes north of the Black Sea.

Right: (A–J) Various types and sizes of Ottoman military tent, and tent-opening systems (after Doras and Kocaman).

(K) Janissary tent decorations. Numbers 2 to 98 are Cemaat units; numbers 1B to 52B are those of Bölük units (after Doras and Kocaman).

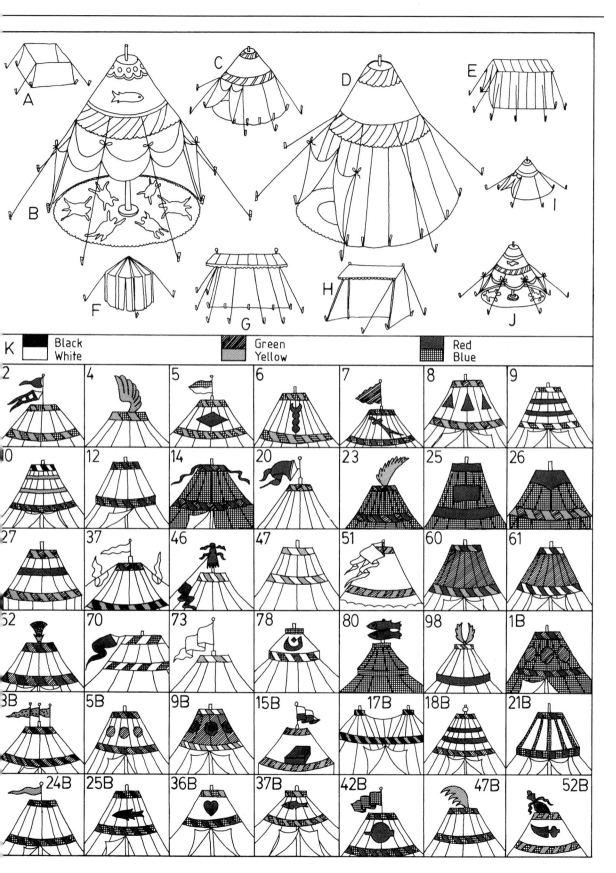

25

An Ottoman army marched at dawn and made camp at noon. Normally a screen of light cavalry scouts and raiders went ahead, followed by a vanguard of elite cavalry, then the main force of infantry and technical troops. The flanks would be covered by the bulk of the cavalry, and a rearguard would protect the baggage. Each Janissary *Orta* had a large tent embroidered with the unit's emblem as its *Oda* or barracks, though each squad seems to have had its own sleeping tent. These were also used during the rare winter campaigns, as in 1644, when the men were at first unable to pitch their tents in the frozen earth. Veteran Janissaries showed them how to tie the guy-ropes to a circle of supply sacks then melt a small patch of earth with boiling water for the tent-pole. Unfortunately the poles were frozen into the earth by morning, and had to be snapped off!

In camp, communal worship was held half an hour before sunset, when the *Orta Imams* recited prayers. Signal cannon were then fired, and the troops would call good fortune and health to their sultan, commander and officers. Vedettes were posted, these being changed to the sound of signal cries and music. Bertrandon de la Broquière, describing a Turkish force leaving camp to meet an enemy early in the 15th century, said: *'When they are ready and know where the Christians are coming and where they are . . ., they leave quickly and in such a manner that a hundred armed Christians would make more noise leaving their camp than ten thousand Turks. All they do is beat a large drum. Those who are supposed to leave get in front and all the rest fall into line, without breaking up the order.'* During the 15th century Ottoman forces also seemed better at re-assembling after a setback than their Christian foes, who, once scattered, tended to go home.

Ottoman tactics evolved over the years but retained certain characteristics. The Janissaries' first major battle was against the Karamanian Turks at Konya in 1389. Here the infantry successfully held the centre, supported by cavalry on the wings and rear. At Ankara in 1402 the infantry adopted a defensive position, holding several hills, and although the battle was eventually lost, the Janissary and *Azap* infantry archers proved themselves capable of repulsing Tamerlane's fearsome cavalry as long as they had cavalry support on their flanks. At Varna in 1444 the Janissaries based their defence on a *tabur* or 'wagenburg' of large carts. It is worth noting that in that instance the small number of men with fire-arms were stationed on the traditionally more defensive left wing. According to the early 16th century Italian observer Paolo Giovio, Ottoman light cavalry tried to draw an enemy into the *Azap* infantry, whereupon both would lure the foe into range of the artillery and Janissaries, while Turkish cavalry hit them in the flanks.

The main offensive role in Ottoman tactics was still given to cavalry, who attempted to break the enemy line. The Janissaries would then fire their guns and attack in a dense mass, with swords and other weapons – usually a single rush in a wedge formation. With a *Mehterhane* band encouraging them from the rear, such massed Janissary charges were often unstoppable, their early effectiveness being due to the fact that their enemies generally lacked disciplined infantry. On the other hand, the Janissaries never used musketry in massed volleys relying instead on individual skills and marksmanship. Elite assault units were known as *Serdengeçti* or 'head riskers', and numbered around 100 volunteers.

The *tabur* or 'wagenburg' has a role in Ottoman history comparable to the circle of covered waggons in America's Wild West. It was probably copied from the Hungarians during the Ottoman conquest of the Balkans. By the late 15th century the Turkish *tabur* consisted of waggons 'like wheeled fortresses' pulled by two mules, and carrying men with matchlocks as well as light cannon. The waggons had ammunition boxes beneath them and could be chained together to make a wall. From the late 17th century, however, the Ottoman *tabur* became increasingly vulnerable to European field artillery.

Ottoman skill in siege warfare stems from even earlier, but two famous sieges stand out in the great era of Ottoman military history: the capture of Constantinople/Istanbul in 1453 and the failed assault on Vienna in 1683. During the former, Ottoman infantry were described by their enemies as disciplined and steady, not attacking in a mad rush but using scaling ladders while archers and hand-gunners kept the defenders' heads down.

The failed attack on Vienna saw the culmination and, in a way, the perfection of traditional Ottoman siege techniques. Their trenches were deeper and broader than had been seen in Western Europe, with musketry batteries at the ends of each sap, as well as assembly points from which attacks were launched. Assaults on the defences were made by day and by night, illuminated by beacons and gunpowder flares, and small *Serdengeçti* units of between 30 and 100 volunteers were sent against limited objectives. The defenders noted that such assault parties were divided into smaller units of five Janissaries: a swordsman, a grenadier, an archer and perhaps two musketeers.

PROMOTION, PAY AND MORALE

Promotions and transfers were done every two to eight years, or on the accession of a new ruler. Within the Janissary Corps these were theoretically by seniority; junior officers were probably selected from the *Çavuş* and *Karakullukçu* NCOs. Discipline was very strict, and it was said that '*forty were led by a single hair*'. Murad I had, in fact, laid down 16 rules for the Janissary Corps: total obedience to officers; unity of purpose; strict military behaviour; no extremes of luxury or abstinence; strict piety under the *Bektaşi* code; acceptance of only the best recruits; capital punishment of a distinctive sort; punishment by only their own officers; promotion by seniority; looking after their own dependants; no beards for ordinary soldiers; no marriage until retirement; living only in barracks; no other trades; full-time military training; and no alcohol or gambling. Punishments varied from imprisonment in the kitchen area (perhaps 'spud bashing') to incarceration in the Dardanelles' fortresses. The most common punishment was hav-

'The siege of Cyprus' in the Şehenşahname of Sultan Selim. While Janissaries march in strict formation on the left, a mixed bag of other Ottoman infantry mill around on the left. Perhaps the artist was making a discreet comment on the discipline of differing formations. (Ms. Ahmet 2595, f.102b, Topkapi Lib., Istanbul)

The late 17th century defences of the Baba Vida castle at Vidin. Inscriptions, recently removed to make the castle 'look more Bulgarian', indicated that the Ottoman governor strengthened these walls in 1723. The inner fortifications date from the 14th century but these Ottoman outer walls and towers were designed for artillery to control the neighbouring Danube river. As such the Baba Vida castle was one of the most important fortifications in Rumelia, the European half of the Ottoman Empire. (Author's photograph)

ing the soles of the feet beaten with a *falaka* or bastinado. After any punishment, the offender had to kiss the hand of his officer as a mark of his return to discipline. Officer punishments ranged from demotion to internal banishment or execution. Discipline on the march was even stricter, with any damage to property being punished, and compensation paid to victims. Desertion in time of war resulted in execution by strangling; the body was then placed in a weighted sack and dropped in the sea or a lake at night to avoid public shame.

Janissaries received their *ulûfe* or pay three or four times a year, paydays often coinciding with visits by foreign dignitaries so as to display Janissary discipline. Bonuses were given for distinguished service,

as when the survivors of *Serdengeçti* ('head-risker') and *Dal Kılıç* ('naked sword') units got extra pay as well as medals. In the mid–15th century ordinary Janissaries received a relatively small amount of money, but they also got enough blue cloth for a pair of trousers, a larger amount of linen, a new woollen coat, a new shirt and enough money to buy bows, arrows and clean collars. Nevertheless the Janissary *Ocak* accounted for ten per cent of total military expenditure which in turn took 15 per cent of the entire Imperial revenue under Mehmet the Conqueror.

In some ways the Janissaries were cushioned from the outside world. Barracks consisted of several *Oda* or rooms for each *Orta* unit, those of the elite being within the Topkapi Palace grounds. Most ordinary barracks consisted of a large building which included kitchens, an arsenal and sleeping quarters; the doors were decorated with the *Orta*'s emblem. The two main barracks in Istanbul, the *Eski* (Old) and the *Yeni* (New) *Oda*, were stone structures built

the 1460s and 1470s – imposing buildings decorated with coloured tiles, marble window-grills,
gilded doors and courtyard fountains. Each also had a
cluster of civilian workshops around it. Here a
janissary lived an almost monastic life, being permitted to marry only when he reached the rank of
oturak or pensioner – at least until the rules were
relaxed at the end of the 16th century.

Generally speaking, ordinary Ottoman soldiers
were more resilient than their Western opponents, a
fact noted by Bertrandon de la Broquière. As he said:
*They are diligent and get up early in the morning. They
are frugal when on the road and live on only a little food,
a little badly baked bread and some raw meat, dried a
little in the sun, or some curdled or otherwise-prepared
milk, some cheese or honey or grapes or fruit or grass, or a
handful of flour from which they make porridge for six or
eight men for a day.'* The Ottoman army also placed
great emphasis on individual courage, and there was
strong competition for 'badges of valour' such as
çelenk crests and feathered plumes; the *çelenk* was
particularly difficult to win as it was only awarded for
extreme bravery in the face of a superior foe. A
soldier killed in battle was a *Şahid* or 'martyr'. His
dependants, like those of any veteran, were known as
odlaharan or 'bread eaters', and were supported by

a special government department through the man's
Orta, being given a weekly food ration, work for sons,
and husbands for daughters. Disabled veterans had
sinecure jobs and remained honorary members of
their *Orta*.

Throughout its history, the Janissary *Ocak* was
popular among the poorest members of society, perhaps because of its almost socialist attitudes which in
turn resulted from the deep influence of the *Bektaşi*
dervish sect. Religion was central to Janissary morale
and motivation, the whole reason for the *Ocak*'s
existence being to expand the power of Islam. But the
Janissaries were hardly orthodox Muslims, and to get
a better idea of their beliefs it is necessary to under-
stand the *Bektaşi* movement.

Bektaşi doctrines contained aspects of ancient
Turkish paganism, Buddhism, a strong element of
Shia Islam – including devotion to the early Caliph
Ali, as well as Kurdish Yazidi (wrongly called 'devil
worshippers') and Christian influences. The latter
include a 'Trinity' of God, the Prophet Muhammad
and the Caliph Ali, belief in confession and absolu-
tion of sins, and an initiation ceremony which involved the distribution of bread, wine and cheese, as
among some Eastern Christians. In many *Bektaşi*
Tekkes or convents, women participated in ceremon-

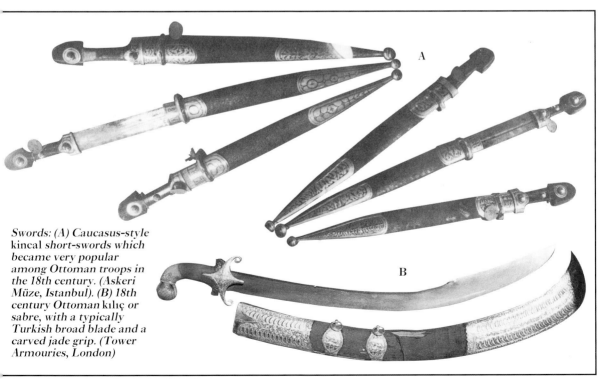

Swords: (A) Caucasus-style kincal short-swords which became very popular among Ottoman troops in the 18th century. (Askeri Müze, Istanbul). (B) 18th century Ottoman kılıç or sabre, with a typically Turkish broad blade and a carved jade grip. (Tower Armouries, London)

The main entrance to the early 16th century Ottoman fort at Muzayrib in southern Syria. A chain of 25 such fortifications protected the Pilgrim road from Damascus to Mecca, each being garrisoned by a small unit of Janissaries or other provincial infantry. (Author's photograph)

Pen and ink drawing of a senior Ottoman officer by Dürer around 1495. German artists started producing accurate representations of Turkish military costume and weaponry soon after Ottoman forces started raiding central Europe. This man's flanged mace, as well as the size of his turban, were a mark of rank or command. (Albertina Coll., no. 3196. D.171, Vienna)

ies without wearing veils. Though the *Bektaşi* movement proclaimed itself part of Sunni Islam, it was certainly not accepted as such by some of the Ottoman establishment. The main difference between the *Bektaşis* and the orthodox Sunni Muslims was a *Bektaşi* belief that, in the final analysis, all religions were valid. Some dervish preachers maintained that Christians and Jews were not really 'infidels', while a few even had Christian followers.

Such opinions appealed to Janissary recruits, whose conversion to Islam resulted, if not from force, at least from moral pressure, and who still sometimes carried Greek or Arabic extracts from the Christian Gospel as lucky charms. It also made the *Bektaşis* popular amongst Balkan Christians, who provided many of the Ottoman Empire's auxiliary infantry. (Their *Tekkes* or convents were especially numerous in places like Albania and Bosnia, where conversion to Islam was widespread and which again would provide some of the Empire's best non-Janissary infantry in the 17th and 18th centuries.) *Bektaşis* fought beside the Janissaries as volunteers. Their attitude to war was summed up in a verse on the blade of a late 15th century axe belonging to a certain Sayyid Ali of Jerusalem:

'*In my hand I took the axe*
As I set out on my journey
Without self-awareness
I became aware of the Beautiful One (God).'

ight *Bektaşis* also lived in the main Janissary barracks. They prayed for victory and walked ahead of the *Yeniçeri Ağası* on parade, their leader chanting *Kerim Allah*' (God is Generous), to which the others responded '*Hu*' (He is). A newly selected *Dede* or head of the *Bektaşi* sect was crowned with a distinctive hat by the *Yeniçeri Ağası* and in turn the *Yeniçeri Ağası* stood whenever the name of Hacci Bektaş, the spiritual father of the sect, was mentioned. The importance of the *Bektaşi* code was reflected, for example, in the discharge paper of Hüseyin, an *Usta* or 'specialist' in the 45th *Bölük* of the 38th *Oda* of the 52th *Orta*, dating from 1822: '*We are believers from of old. We have confessed the Unity of Reality. We have a Prophet, Ahmeti Muhtar Cenap. Since the time of the Heroes we have been the intoxicated ones. We are the Moths of the Divine Flame. We are a company of wandering dervishes in this world. We cannot be counted on the fingers, we cannot be destroyed by defeat . . .*'

SUPPORT SERVICES AND OTHER DUTIES

The most important support services within the Janissary *Ocak* were the *Cebecis* or 'armourers' and the *Saka* or 'water-distributers', the latter accompanying soldiers into battle and tending the wounded. The *Cebecis* made, repaired and issued weapons and also formed a fully operational unit. In 1574 they were a small elite of 625 skilled men attached to the artillery, but later their numbers were greatly increased, till all large garrisons included some *Cebecis*.

Non-combatant support personnel within the *Ocak* included 100 *Yazıcı* or 'scribes' led by the *Yeniçeri Kâtibi* or 'secretary of Janissaries' and the apparently separate *Oda Yazıcı* or 'barrack-room scribes' who, under a *Baş Yazıcı* ('head clerk'), looked after an *Orta*'s paperwork. Then there was the *Kârhane*, originally consisting of 34 small companies of skilled artisans under an *Usta* or 'master'. The *Kârhane* went on campaign and enjoyed some of the privileges of the Janissary *Ocak*. These civilian craft or business guilds rapidly increased in number and became known as the *Ordu Esnaf* or army artisans.

Ottoman forces overrunning the outer defences of a powerful river-fortress on the Austrian frontier, from the Süleymanname of 1558. The techniques of river warfare were vital in Hungary, as they were in southern Russia. They were also an area in which Janissaries excelled. (Ms. Haz. 1517, Topkapi Lib., Istanbul)

Eventually, an Ottoman army on a major campaign would be followed by wool carvers, sword makers, bow makers, saddlers, linen drapers, cobblers, barbers, blacksmiths, candle makers, cooked sheep's head sellers, iron shoe-heel makers, pharmacists, goat's hair cloth makers, slipper makers, kaftan makers, silk merchants, trouser makers, copper-smiths, tin smiths and bakers, among others. By the 18th century they occupied a permanent position, and most also claimed to be Janissaries, demanding full pay.

Another distinctive characteristic of the Ottoman army was its *Mehterhane* or military band; the Ottoman Empire was first in Europe to have a permanent military music organisation. A *Mehterhane* consisted of 'folds', each normally with a drum, doubled kettle drums, clarinet, trumpet and cymbals. The Sultan's own band had nine such folds, the *Yeniçeri Ağası*'s seven, and every regiment or garrison had a smaller band. A *Mehterhane* usually stood in a crescent formation; only the kettle-drummer sat. Large *Kös* or war-drums were often played on camel-back, and a *Mehterhane* could also be entirely mounted. The instruments were made and maintained by 150–200 specialists, mostly Greeks or Armenians based near the Topkapı Palace. (The *Çevgani* singers who are still such a tourist attraction in Istanbul were not added to the *Mehterhane* until the late 18th century.) The *Mehterhane* played 'tunes of Afrasiyab', in other words Persian military music, and according to the colourful Turkish traveller Evliya Çelebi in 1638: '. . . *five hundred trumpeters raised such a sound that the planet Venus began to dance and the skies reverberated . . . All these players of the drum, kettle-drum and cymbals marched past together beating their different kinds of instruments in rhythmic unison as if Chama-Pur's army* [the traditional foe of Alexander the Great] *was marching by.*'

Ottoman infantry forces had duties apart from fighting. In winter the Janissaries worked on building

sites, the middle ranking *Amelimanda* being responsible for maintaining Istanbul's vital aqueduct system. With such training the Janissaries were, not surprisingly, effective sappers on campaign. From the star infantry garrisoned newly conquered towns; th Janissaries usually took over citadels, while *Aza* occupied the town beneath. The citadels and fort resses would then be well stocked with food an ammunition, so the occupying Janissaries coul rarely be starved into submission. However, the Ot tomans did not put much emphasis on fortification until the latter part of the 16th century, when thei frontiers began to stabilise.

By then much of the Janissary *Ocak* was sprea across the Empire in *Korocu* (garrison) *Ortas* whic normally did nine-month tours of duty before re turning to the capital. But as the Corps grew, th majority of its *Ortas* became permanently based i the provinces, under the command of local gover nors. They developed local interests, local loyaltie sometimes taking over local administration, an eventually they became a source of unrest them selves. Meanwhile *Yamak* volunteer auxiliaries dubious military value were left to garrison the vit Bosphorus fortresses by the 18th century.

Different forms of provincial garrison develope within the Empire. For example, the *Hükûme Sancak* or 'autonomous hereditary provinces' of east ern Anatolia were governed by tribal princes sup ported by Janissary *Ortas*. In Iraq and Syria th Janissaries became local elites. The descendants the first garrisons were assimilated into the Arab speaking population and became fierce rivals of late *Ortas* sent to reinforce central government contro The large Ottoman army based in Egypt similarl developed a form of local patriotism, but the Egyp tian *Ortas* remained loyal to the Empire and cam paigned far from home, fighting in Italy (1619–20 Yemen (1631–2) and Armenia (winter 1616). Eve the small Ottoman-held areas of Eritrea, Yemen an the Arabian Gulf coast had small garrisons, while th

'Ottoman army commanded by Ferhat Paşa approaching the fortress of Revan', from the Şehenşahname *by Loqman, 1594–97. Officers with tall Janissary caps ride amid dense ranks of Janissary soldiers. Baggage* camels fill the lower part of the picture, and there i a mounted **Mehterhane** band hidden among massed cavalry behind th Janissaries. (Ms. Baghdad 200, f.101b, Topkapi Lib., Istanbul)

The early days
1: Nefer Janissary soldier,
   late 14th century
2: Byzantine officer,
   early 15th century
3: Turkish Yaya infantryman,
   14th century

Recruitment and education
1: Devşirme recruit, 16th century
2: Enderum Sakirdi eunuch teacher
3: Civelek young trainee off-duty

B

3   1   2

Training
1: Acemi Oğlan Janissary trainee,
   early 16th century
2: İç Oğlan Çavuşu NCO of new
   Janissary recruits, 17th century
3: Falakacı Başı head of punishment unit,
   17th-18th centuries

C

Janissary soldiers

1: Zırhlı Nefer armoured soldier, 16th century
2: Kesıcı Silahkarda Müsellah Janissary archer, early 16th century
3: Yanıcı Silahkarda Müsellah Janissary musketeer, early 16th century

D

Janissary junior officers
1: Serdengecti Ağa commander of an assault unit, 18th century
2: Bayraktar Subayı standard bearer of 39th Orta, 16th century
3: Beşinci Karakullukçu NCO, 18th century

2   3   1   E

Janissary officers
1: Usta officer, 17th-18th centuries
2: Başçavuş officer of third rank, 16th-18th centuries
3: Kethüda Bey officer

Commanding officers
1: Yeniçeri Ağası Commander of
    the Janissary corps
2: Orta Kethüdasi Janissary officer
3: Haseki Ağası Commander of the Sultan's infantry guard, 18th century

Religious support
1: Orta Imam battalion chaplain
2: Bektaşi dervish
3: Kulluk of the Ellialtı Neferi patrolman of 56th Orta, 18th century

H   2   3   1

Mehter Military Band
1: Mehterbaşı Ağa conductor
2: Zurnazen clarinet player
3: Mehter Ağası of Köszen, leader of kettle-drum section

2   3   1   I

Support personnel
1: Aşçı cook
2: Orta Sakası battalion water-carrier
3: Bostancı Aşçısı 'cook' junior officer
   of a Bostancı battalion
4: Woman from Mitilini, 16th century

J   2   4   1   3

The Bostancı Corps
1: Bostancı Binbaşı, 18th century
2: Bostancı Nefer soldier of the 3rd rank, 17th century
3: Bostancı Kethüdası officer

1   3   2   **K**

Other infantry forces
1: Levent, late 16th century
2: Azap, 16th-17th century
3: Sekbanbaşı officer of
   the Sekban corps

L   1   2   3

rtually independent Ottoman provinces of North frica raised their own Janissary *Ocaks*.

The Janissaries' public order duties eventually came more important than their military role. The *eniçeri Ağası* was, for example, also chief of police of e capital; his own Janissaries and those of the *ebecıbaşı* and the *Topçubaşı* patrolled Istanbul and alata, and *Bostancıs* policed the surrounding areas. these units went on campaign, the *Acemi Oğlan rta* or 'training battalions' sometimes took over licing.

A unit of 300 men was used to protect a fleet of) to 100 transport boats on the rivers Morava and isava, based at Nis. Janissaries had always served oard Ottoman warships, and by the early 17th ntury most Ottoman galleys seem to have carried ght Janissaries and six other soldiers, mostly recuited on the Aegean islands and armed with atchlocks, bows and a few light cannon. Janissaries marine duty were normally drawn from the older, ore experienced but less fit *Oturak* or 'pensioner' ade, while other marines included *Sipahis* (supposly 'feudal cavalry'), *Kur'acı* or 'conscripts' and *lûfeci* or 'salaried' soldiers. Far to the west, in giers, a virtually separate Janissary *Ocak* provided e powerbase for famous corsairs like Hayruddin rbarossa. They were initially raised to defend giers and extend Ottoman control, but they soon sisted on taking part in the profitable business of val warfare – or piracy, as their European foes lled it.

OTHER INFANTRY FORCES

The first, but also among the most short-lived, Ottoman infantry formations were the early 14th century *Yaya* and *Piyade*. The former were Turks given land in return for military service and local defence duties in Rumelia (the Balkans), the latter comparable soldier-farmers in Anatolia, though they also included nomads. The *Yaya* were commanded by *Çerıbaşı* or 'soldier leaders' under the command of tribal *Yürük Begs* and provincial governors. They were organised into rudimentary *Ocak* units of around 30 men each, five of whom served in rotation while the others supported them financially. The idea that these *Yaya* were grouped into decimal units is probably a myth.

The *Azap* or 'bachelors' were a more successful formation which became a fierce rival of the elite Janissary *Ocak*. An *Azap* was a volunteer, originally recruited from Anatolian Turks, paid only during a campaign and able to leave whenever he wished. Large numbers of *Azaps* served as marines in various Turkish *Beyliks* during the 14th century. They were armed with maces, bows (often shooting *zemberek* short darts with the aid of arrow-guides), and occasionally *çagra* crossbows; and they soon adopted *tüfek* guns. According to the Byzantine chronicler Dukas, the first Ottoman garrison at Gallipoli in

ıe of the best-preserved ttoman fortresses is at ıyas, overlooking the ılf of Iskenderun. It was ilt by Selim I early in e 16th century to protect ulnerable stretch of the ad from Istanbul to ria which was exposed naval raids at this point. ıe structure is a typical ttoman fortress, being nctional rather than signed to impress or ıke a political ıtement. (Author's ıotograph)

1421–22 consisted of '*lightly armed Gasmouli*', indi cating soldiers of mixed Greek and Western Euro pean origin. Ottoman records still referred to tw units of Greek-speaking Muslims at Gallipoli 1474, probably *Azaps* rather than Janissaries. On consisted of rowers, the other of *Zenberekcıyan* arch ers who defended the castle. Four other, presumab Turkish, units at Gallipoli included a unit of nav *Azaps*.

On land, the *Azaps* fought as infantry archers b were mostly employed as guards or pickets. By th 16th century they had declined to mere ammuniti carriers, pioneers and sappers, and had been a sorbed into the Janissaries *Cebeci* as porters. The however, the *Azaps* enjoyed a new lease of life. Fro the late 16th century all Muslim men in frontie regions were liable to be enlisted as *Azaps*, arme with matchlocks and sabres, one man from each 20 30 households being supported by the rest. Th were divided into *Kale Azapı* ('fortress *Azaps*') an

Janissaries and their officers approach the Sultan's tent while on campaign, from the Süleymanname of 1558. A row of triple-horsehair

Tuğs stand inside a tented enclosure which is made to look like a fortress. (Ms. Haz. 1517, Topkapi Lib., Istanbul)

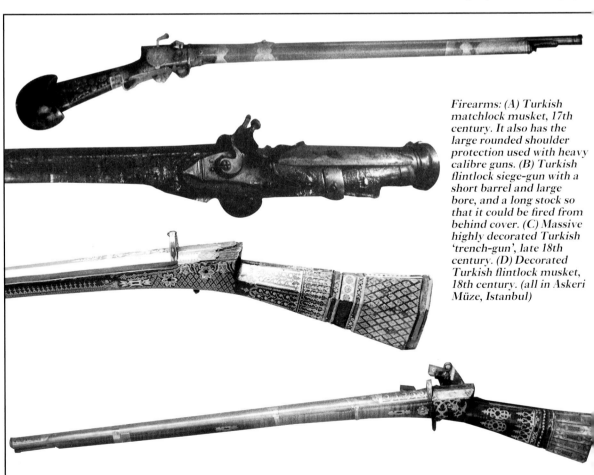

Firearms: (A) Turkish matchlock musket, 17th century. It also has the large rounded shoulder protection used with heavy calibre guns. (B) Turkish flintlock siege-gun with a short barrel and large bore, and a long stock so that it could be fired from behind cover. (C) Massive highly decorated Turkish 'trench-gun', late 18th century. (D) Decorated Turkish flintlock musket, 18th century. (all in Askeri Müze, Istanbul)

Deniz Azapi ('naval *Azaps*') depending on where they lived. It is not clear whether auxiliary infantry known as *Cânbâzân* ('soul stakers') or *Dîvânegân* ('Madmen') were *Azaps* – such titles were probably descriptive rather than references to specific units.

The history of the *Voynuqs* is even more varied. Essentially they were auxiliaries recruited from the Ottoman Empire's Balkan Christian vassals, under a system inherited from pre-Turkish times, though they do seem to have included Muslims from early on. Most were armoured cavalry, but again they included some foot soldiers. Their ranks were largely Slav Bulgarians and Serbs, as well as Vlach- or Rumanian-speakers. Like many Ottoman auxiliaries, a *Voynuq* was supported by other households known as *Gönder*, a term probably stemming from the Greek word *Kontarion* or lance. The *Voynuqs* had their own *Ceribaşı* officers under the overall command of the *Voynuq Beyi*, and were attended by *Yamak* servants or subordinates. Although the *Voynuqs* had no *Ocak* or corps structure they included a registered reserve which kept them up to strength. By the 15th century some *Voynuqs* had additional duties such as looking after herds of cavalry horses in Bulgaria. The *Dogancis* ('hawkers') were similar to these *Voynuqs* and raised hawks for the Imperial Court. Elsewhere Vlach Christian nomads enjoyed special privileges in return for serving the Ottoman Empire as frontier *Voynuqs*, guides, guards and raiders. The autonomous Rumanian principality of Moldavia also supplied *Voynuqs* during the 16th century.

The role of infantry in the Rumanian principalities sheds an interesting light on a little-known aspect of Ottoman military organisation. Because Moldavia, Wallachia and Transylvania preserved their autonomy for so long, their pre-Ottoman military heritage continued to develop. In all three parts of what is now Rumania, local rulers raised, trained and equipped competent infantry as the Ottoman tide approached. These infantry ranged from professional Italian mercenaries to revitalised urban militias stiffened by royal garrisons. They used the normal array of late medieval infantry weapons, including a hooked staff for use against cavalry, a device soon adopted by the Janissaries. At the same time, infantry archers armed with Asiatic-style composite bows were gradually replaced by musketeers skilled in guerrilla warfare. In fact Wallachia and Moldavia continued to recruit professional arquebus-armed infantry from Christian Bulgarians to the south, Serbs to the west, Poles and Cossacks to the north. Ottoman military influence was also felt, for example in a *Dorubanti* infantry militia based on the Turkish *Derbentçi* or 'frontier guards'.

The Ottoman Empire inherited several other interesting military formations in the southern Balkans; for example, ex-Byzantine Catalan mercenaries or their descendants were recorded in Ottoman service in the 1380s. Vassal or mercenary European crossbowmen and axe-armed Genoese infantry from various colonial outposts were among those involved in the Ottoman civil war of 1421–22. Jews and Muslims joined in defeating an Italian attack on the island of Chios in 1599, since only they and not the local Greek Christians were permitted inside the

'Mustafa Paşa giving a feast for the Janissaries', from the Nusretname *by Mustafa Ali, 1584. Janissaries with flat-topped* Börks *and officers with tall pointed* Üsküfs *are served by splendidly dressed court attendants and members of the Sultan's Silâhtar guard. (Ms. Haz. 1365, f.33v, Topkapi Lib., Istanbul)*

swords and daggers, and were led by hereditar[y] *Kapitanos*. Senior Greek religious figures were per[-]mitted their own *Kapoi* armed retainers. *Müsellem* were originally a cavalry levy, and though they de[-]clined into an ineffective infantry militia, they re[-]tained some kind of *Ocak* Corps structure. Th[e] *Gönüllüyan* were a later volunteer militia of horse[-]men and foot soldiers raised from both Muslims an[d] Christians, paid through local taxes and used t[o] garrison local castles.

For many years the Ottoman government tried t[o] stop the *Raya*, or non-military section of the popula[-]tion, from acquiring firearms. Even the recognise[d] *Derbentçi* auxiliaries were not permitted guns until a[n] increasing threat from gun-toting bandits made thi[s] essential. Properly organised Ottoman *Derbentçis* ap[-]peared in the mid-15th century, and initially in[-]cluded Christian *Martolos* as well as *Yörük* Turkis[h] nomads, Turcoman tribesmen from Anatolia an[d] Balkan Christian *Voynuqs*. They were organised in[to] units of between 25 and 30 local men garrisoning tin[y] forts in strategic or vulnerable areas, and this syste[m]

'Kan'an Paşa marching against Albanian rebels', from the Paşaname of c.1630. The only Janissaries in this picture appear to act as the Paşa's immediate guard. In front of the commander are axe-armed troops, perhaps Levents, but the majority of the infantry appear to be Tüfekçi musketeers with short red coats and tall red caps. (British Lib., Ms. Sl. 3584, f.20a, London)

island's citadel. Far to the north, many of the perse-cuted Bogomil 'heretics' of Bosnia also helped the invading Ottomans against their Christian oppres-sors.

Elsewhere the Ottomans used existing local forces as garrison troops to avoid tying down their own soldiers. The Greek *Martolos*, for example, were originally Byzantine irregulars. In the early 15th century the Ottomans recognised them as *Nizam* or 'proper soldiers', and paid them to control *Klepht* Greek mountain bandits. During the 16th century *Martolos* formed a significant element in garrisons across Serbia, Bosnia, Herzegovina and even Hun-gary. By the 18th century they had muskets, pistols,

The castle outside Uzice in western Serbia was one of the strongest fortifications in the Ottoman Eyâlet of Bosnia. The position is so powerful that it was reused by Axis occupation forces during the Second World War. (Author's photograph)

'Procession of the Ottoman Sultan's sons in a Carriage', a double-page picture from the Surname of Vehbi, 1650–85. The carriage is escorted by a variety of soldiers including Solak guardsmen with decorated bronze helmets, Janissary officers with enormously plumed Üsküf hats, Bostancıs wearing long floppy red hats and Silâhtars with red versions of the Janissary Börk. (Ms. Ahmet A.3593, ff.169v-170r, Topkapi Lib., Istanbul)

ould be greatly expanded as the authority of the entral government waned. *Derbentçis* were even und in the autonomous Crimean Tatar Khanate, orth of the Black Sea. The Crimean Tatars also elded a small musket-armed infantry force. Some ere tribesmen too poor to own a horse; others rmed an elite of 20 companies of mounted infantry *ekbans* recruited from villagers in the Crimean eninsula.

The increasing conservatism of Ottoman mili- ry thinking ensured that when a new infantry force as raised it was given a traditional name. As a result, ie *Sekban* infantry of the late 16th to 18th centuries ad no real connection with the old *Sekban* division f the Janissary *Ocak*. The new *Sekbans* were an iswer to the Ottoman army's acute shortage of usket troops in the face of ever-stronger European iemies. The supposedly non-military Muslim *Raya* opulations of Dalmatia, Albania, Bosnia and natolia were now recruited in increasing numbers, any as mounted infantry. Early in the 17th century ie new *Sekbans* were organised on a regular basis in *ölük* units of between 50 and 100 men, mostly paid

as private armies by provincial governors. Each unit was led by a *Bölük Başı* under the overall command of a *Baş Bölük Başı*, such officers at first being drawn from the Janissary *Ocak*. Theoretically they could be disbanded when their *Bölüm* or commission was withdrawn, but in reality they were rarely under central government control. Eventually they became the most effective infantry in the Empire, outstrip- ping the decadent Janissaries. Other similar units were known as *Sarıca* or 'wasps', and all tended to be excellent marksmen, perhaps because so many had been huntsmen or bandits before becoming soldiers.

Like the *Sekbans* and *Sarıca*, the revived *Levent* forces of the late 16th century were Muslims armed with muskets, swords and, later, pistols. They were supposedly recruited from bandits in Anatolia and

seem to have had no connection with earlier *Leve[*
marines of the 14th century. Another new force wer[
the mounted infantry, the *Tüfekçis*, who appeared i[
the 16th century and became some of the mo[
effective troops in the 17th and 18th century Otto[
man army. They, however, were a regular corp[
uniformed in short red coats and tall red caps.

Savage incursions by Catholic Austrian armie[
meant that in many parts of the Balkans, Orthodo[
Christians still gave military help to the beleaguere[
Ottomans. Even fiercer resistance was put up by th[
Slav-speaking Muslims of Bosnia, where distin[
types of local infantry, such as the *Panduk* or 'shar[
shooters' and the *Eflak* or 'musketeers', appeared. I[
Syria and Iraq an extraordinary array of irregular an[
mercenary formations appeared during the 17th an[
18th centuries. In Damascus these included *Leven[*
mounted infantry who were at first Turks but late[
tended to be Kurds, *Sekban* – Turks from easter[
Anatolia, *Maghâriba* – Algerian Arabs who wer[
generally employed to defend Pilgrim Caravans t[
Mecca, and *Tüfekçi* – Kurds who formed a small eli[
of marksmen. Each had their own organisation, co[
porate loyalty, leadership, barracks and distinctiv[
clothing. In addition there were *'Ashir* – Syria[
auxiliaries under tribal or local leaders, includin[
urban militias raised from all religious groups. Th[
term *Arab*, however, was only used of bedouin auxi[

'Battle between Ottoman and Imperial Hapsburg forces', in the Khamseh of Ata'i *of c. 1675. The Janissaries are armed with curved sabres, though one soldier is also wrestling with his enemy. (Ms. Revan 816, f.10, Topkapi Lib., Istanbul)*

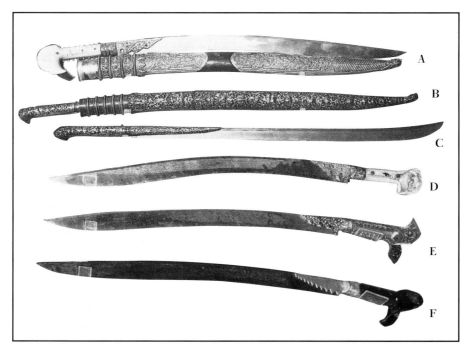

Yatağan reverse-curved single-edged swords. Such weapons were characteristic of Ottoman troops, both regular and tribal auxiliaries: (A–C) Three late 18th century Yatağans with highly decorated scabbards. (Tower Armouries, London). (D–F) Three plainer yatağans showing their large hook-like pommels. (Askeri Müze, Istanbul)

ries who had an important military role east of the ...rontes, Litani and Jordan rivers.

The situation in Egypt was generally more ...eaceful, though rivalry between different units of-...n boiled over into rioting. There were seven corps ...the Cairo garrison, plus assorted irregular forma-...ons which, in the Arabic records, were known as: ...nissaries, *Azaps*, *Sarrâj* (*Sarıca*), *Yuldâsh* (from ...*oldaş* or Janissary soldier), *Maghribi* irregulars, ...*mâkiya* (from *Yamak*, a Janissary's servant), ...*ufenkjiya*, *Jarâkisa* (from *Yürük*, Turkish tribes-...en), *Shâwûshiya* (from *Çavuş*, Janissary sergeants), ...*Mutafarriqa* (from the *Müteferrika*, Ottoman Palace ...uardsmen), and *Gönüllü* or 'volunteers' who were ...erhaps still recognisably Turks. In times of tension ...he smaller units tended to ally with the *Azaps* ...gainst the dominant Janissaries. In North Africa the ...nissaries, though forming a separate *Ocak* Corps, ...tained their Turkish identity for several centuries. ...heir great rivals were the *Tâ'ifat al Ru'sâ* or 'mili-...as of the corsair captains' who were basically ma-...nes. These *Tâ'ifat al Ru'sâ* included some Turks, ...ut the majority were indigenous North African ...rabs and Berbers.

...Janissary Orta's cooking ...ot or Kazan was the unit's ...ost prized possession ...nd would be carried in ...eremonial processions.

It was accompanied by an equally symbolic oversized soup ladle. (Askeri Müze, Istanbul)

THE PLATES

Plate A: The early days
A1: Nefer Janissary soldier, late 14th century
No Turkish illustrations of Janissaries are known from the 14th century, so this figure is based on written descriptions and 'enemy' pictures of Otto-mans. He is equipped as an infantry archer but still wears a fluted 'turban-helmet' and a mail hauberk beneath his *Dolama* coat. He uses a *siper* or 'arrow-guide' for shooting short darts – a device which superseded the medieval *majra* arrow-guide. The long quiver could be opened down its entire length, and is of a type used in Turkish-influenced parts of eastern Europe. The sword is a European import suspended in a Middle Eastern manner.

A2: Byzantine officer, early 15th century
Late Byzantine military costume owed nothing to the Roman heritage. This reconstruction is based on Balkan wall-paintings and a painted Italian chest showing Turks and Byzantines, almost certainly based on sketches brought back by itinerant Italian artists. Among several distinctive features are a shield of Italo-Balkan form, a sword of Byzantine type and a flanged mace of eastern European form. The tall yellow felt hat was a style common on both sides of the late Byzantine-Muslim frontier.

A3: Turkish Yaya infantryman, 14th century
This figure is based on a mixture of Turco-Iranian manuscript illustrations and written descriptions.

The türbe *or tomb of the famous* Bektaşi *dervish shaykh,* Gül Baba, *on a hillside overlooking Budapest. Like many other* Bektaşis, *Gül Baba ('Father of Roses') is said to have accompanied the Janissaries during the capture of Budapest in 1526. He died there on 2 September 1541 and his spirit was regarded as protector of the city during the 145 years of Ottoman rule. The türbe itself was built between 1543 and 1548, becoming something of a pilgrimage site for the local Janissary garrison. (Author's photograph)*

His basic costume is that of a 14th–15th century Turkish nomad, typical features being the segmented felt hat. As a foot soldier he also has the laced gaiters of an Anatolian or Iranian peasant. Some *Yaya* and *Azap* infantry used crossbows, but no pictorial evidence survives, so this soldier has been given captured Hungarian crossbow equipment.

Plate B: Recruitment and education
B1: Devşirme recruit, 16th century
Once the Janissary *Ocak* was fully developed, its uniforms barely changed for 300 years. The most famous illustration of a *Devşirme* levy shows boy recruits all in red, with what looks like simple red versions of the Janissary cap. They also seem to have been allowed to keep one small bag of personal possessions.

B2: Enderum Sakirdi eunuch teacher
The senior teachers of the elite *Iç Oğlanı* or 'student pages' were eunuchs, mostly of European origin. They formed a well-educated and highly respected corps within the *Kapıkullu* – the sultan's own serv-

ants, which also included the Janissary Corps. The distinctive uniform included a very tall hat with narrow turban-cloth, but instead of weapons the carried a combined pen-case and ink-well, her thrust into the man's belt.

B3: Civelek young trainee off-duty
A *Civelek* was a recruit recently promoted into th ranks of a fighting *Orta*. His uniform was essentiall that of an ordinary Janissary soldier. Here he wears short jacket, probably a *Mintan*, with a *yatağa* reverse-curved sword. The *Civelek* has a tall turbar perhaps indicating that he is not fully entitled to wea a Janissary *Börk* cap, but with one of the fringed end hanging in front of his face. This appears in Turkis sources, and may reflect the younger soldiers' ten dency to fool around – hence their name, *Civele* meaning 'lively' or 'playful'.

Plate C: Training
C1: Acemi Oğlan Janissary trainee, early 16th century
A Janissary's training was long, hard and serious; tha of an ordinary *Acemi Oğlan* was entirely militar This young man would appear to be in off-dut dress, wearing a *Hırka* jacket with short, flare sleeves. His felt hat would be conical in shape but ha been tipped forward. Hanging from his belt or thru into his sash in his musketry equipment: a ba containing bullets, lead bars and a bullet-mould, powder horn, a priming flask and a small axe to cu lead for casting as bullets.

C2: Iç Oğlan Çavuşu NCO of new Janissary recruits, 17th century
Officer ranks were largely indicated by their head gear. This *Çavuş* 'sergeant' wears a small turbar cloth around a *Kavuğ* hat with a vertically quilte surface. His double-breasted *cübbe* coat is tucke inside *şalvar* baggy trousers and he has a fine gol and ivory dagger. The most distinctive object is th *çevgen*, a chain of small bells on a staff used both t mark time when marching and as a mark of office.

C3: Falakacı Başı head of punishment unit, 17th–18th centuries
Few officers can have been as feared as the *Falaka Başı*, whose squad was responsible for maintainin

order in the *Orta*. Here he wears a large turban (the size of which indicated his authority), with his *takke* skull-cap just visible. His *kaftan* coat is tucked through a *kuşak* or sash to show his long *entari* 'shirt'. In addition to a *yatağan*, he carries two *falaka* bastinados of different weights in a large container.

Plate D: Janissary soldiers

D1: Zırhli Nefer armoured soldier, 16th century

Janissaries who continued to wear full armour were simply known as *Zırhli Nefer* or 'armoured soldiers'. They were used as assault troops, and probably formed part of the *Serdengeçti* 'head risker' elite. This man has a highly decorated gilded helmet with a Janissary plume-holder on the front, a flexible neck-guard and a mail-and-plate *zırh gömlek* or cuirass. The latter, like his *demir dizçek* thigh and knee protections, was more commonly used by cavalry by the 16th century. His shield is a form adopted from the Ottoman's eastern European foes, while the *tırpan* staff-weapon suggests Italian influence.

D2: Kesıcı Silahkarda Müsellah Janissary archer, early 16th century

Janissary assault squads also included archers, perhaps because muskets took so long to reload. This

*bove: 'The death of Gül ‘aba in Budapest, 1541'; ainting by Şükrü Erdiren. ‘he Baba's disciple tanding on the left has *any of the symbolic or *itual objects associated ith the* Bektaşi *order. *skeri Müze, Istanbul)*

Skirmish between *ttomans and Russians', * the* Shaja’atname *of *safi Paşa, late 17th-early *th century. The *nissaries have their *nics tucked up into their *elts, perhaps ready to *ursue a fleeing Russian *ule handler. Below them *wo dismounted Turkish *orse-archers shoot at * ussian musketeers. (Ms. *ildiz 2385/105, vol. IV, *182, Istanbul University *ib.)*

man's kit includes elements that later dropped out of use or changed. For example, his *Börk* cap is lower than was seen later and his *dolama* jacket has embroidery around the shoulders. The soldier also carries a crude wooden siege mantlet, as shown in several manuscript illustrations.

D3: Yanıcı Silahkarda Müsellah Janissary musketeer, early 16th century
The third element in a Janissary assault unit consisted of musketeers. Here they are carrrying the massive 'trench-gun' so feared by the Ottomans' enemies. The engraved brass band and empty plume-holder suggest that he was a member of an elite or palace-based *Orta*. In addition to a bullet-pouch, powder-horn, priming-flask, small axe and long knife, he carries a straight-bladed sword with a sabre-hilt, perhaps a *gaddara* or a *pala*.

Plate E: Janissary junior officers
E1: Serdengectı Ağa commander of an assault unit, 18th century
In common with elite forces in all armies, the *Serdengeçtı* or 'head-riskers' seem to have worn more extravagant uniforms than ordinary soldiers. As a senior officer this man also has a rakish turban rather than an ordinary Janissary *Börk*, while various parts of his costume are embroidered and fur-trimmed. His polished brass belt is of an elaborate type, and the metallic hoops around his legs may be decorations attached to garters. The officer also carries a horse-hair *Tuğ* – the banner of his unit or *Orta*.

E2: Bayraktar Subayı standard bearer of 39th Orta, 16th century
A tall *Üsküf* cap was the badge of commissione officers in the Janissary *Ocak*. Here it is worn withou the huge plumes worn on parade. The *dolama* coa has false sleeves, the wearer's arms coming throug slits in front of the armpits. This officer carries *Bayrak* or banner bearing the double-bladed *Dhu Faqqar* or 'Sword of Ali', a device adopted by sever: Janissary units.

E3: Beşinci Karakullukçu NCO, 18th century
The *Beşinci Karakullukçu* was the senic *Karakullukçu* 'scullion' NCO in a Janissary unit. B the 18th century many troops no longer wore prope Janissary *Börk* hats but sported flamboyant turban: as well as impractical extensions to their fur-line jackets, suggesting that they were no longer fightin soldiers. They still carried swords or daggers, gener ally of the *yatağan* type shown here. The massiv long-bladed axe with a thrusting point was, howeve still a common infantry weapon.

Plate F: Janissary officers
F1: Usta officer, 17th–18th centuries
Janissary officer uniform was often elaborate, and th fact that captured examples are found in centr: European museums suggests that such dress wa worn on campaign. In addition to his ordinar Janissary *Börk* hat with its plume, this *Usta* c 'master' has the tooled and stained leather coat asso ciated with his status. It probably developed from

The fortress known as Ak Kirman in Turkish, Bilgorod Dnistrovskiy in Ukrainian, and Cetatea Alba in Rumanian; all mean 'White Castle'. The oldest parts date from the 14th–15th centuries and were built by the Genoese or Moldavians, the outer walls being erected by the Moldavians and Ottoman in the 15th–17th centuries It was one of the strongest Ottoman military bases north of the Black Sea. (Odessa Archaeological Museum, Ukraine)

ather tunic worn by cooks and could reflect the culinary origins of many Janissary ranks. Beneath the coat is a decorated leather apron with a brass fringe.

G2: Başçavuş officer of third rank, 16th–18th centuries

As a more senior officer, the *Başçavuş* wears an even more elaborate uniform, including a huge feather plume thrust into the front of his strangely folded *Üsküf* hat. His coat has false sleeves that are so long they are crossed behind his back and then tossed over his shoulders. The almost transparent shirt that hangs beneath his *kaftan* was reserved for officers of elite units or for those who served close to the Sultan.

G3: Kethüda Bey officer

The *Börk* Janissary cap of this officer is turned to the side and pinned in place with a plume-holder that might be a *çelenk* gallantry medal. He wears a fur-rimmed *tennure*, a garment originally associated with dervishes, and beneath it a coat with puffed sleeves (a fashion that became increasingly popular in the period) and a long cotton *gömlek* shirt. As a senior officer serving in the Palace, he is also entitled to wear yellow rather than red shoes.

Plate G: Commanding officers
G1: Yeniçeri Ağası Commander of the Janissary Corps

The official costume of the *Yeniçeri Ağası* was similar than that of some lesser officers, though his clothes would have been of the finest fabric. He was distinguished by an abundance of expensive fur, a large turban and highly decorated weapons, some were being held by an assistant. The gilded and enamelled mace is a symbolic weapon indicating the *Ağa*'s rank, and the elaborate *cicik*, the breast-shaped gilded copper helmet, would have given little real protection.

G2: Orta Kethüdası Janissary officer

Whether the two plumes in this officer's hat indicate rank or gallantry is unknown. His uniform is similar to that of a number of middle-ranking staff officers, and includes very long, false sleeves, which are crossed behind his back. The close similarity among uniforms suggests that headgear was the most important indication of status and role; perhaps also that

'Jugglers and acrobats in the Ok Meydan', from the Surname-i Vehbi of c.1720–30. By the 18th century the Janissary Ocak had declined from its earlier military prowess but was still used to police the streets of major cities like Istanbul. Here Janissaries form a cordon around the kind of traditional Turkish entertainers that were famous as far afield as Italy and Russia. (Ms. Ahmet 3593, f.84a, Topkapi Lib., Istanbul)

some ranks were the same in seniority but differed in function.

G3: Haseki Ağası Commander of the Sultan's infantry guard, 18th century

This figure again indicates how Janissary uniforms became more elaborate as the fighting capability of the Janissary *Ocak* declined. An interesting – and perhaps new – fashion was the flat-topped *fes* or 'fez', with a dark tassle on top. This was of Byzantine Greek rather than Turkish origin, and was to become the uniform hat of the Ottoman army during the 19th century. In addition to a leather briefcase for official papers and a decorated leather water-bottle, this senior officer is armed with a dagger, a *yatağan* sword and a Turkish flintlock musket.

Plate H: Religious support
H1: Orta Imam battalion chaplain

Religious support in the Janissary *Ocak* was more like that seen in the Protestant north rather than the Catholic south of Europe because of its simplicity and lack of pomp. This was reflected in the plain uniform worn by the senior *Ocak Imam* and his staff of *Orta Imams*. Only the *Imam*'s simple green *Külâh* hat, with its small, neat turban, and perhaps his beard indicated his religious role. The Muslim Holy Book, or *Qur'an*, was kept dust-free in a cloth bag and carried in the leather satchel.

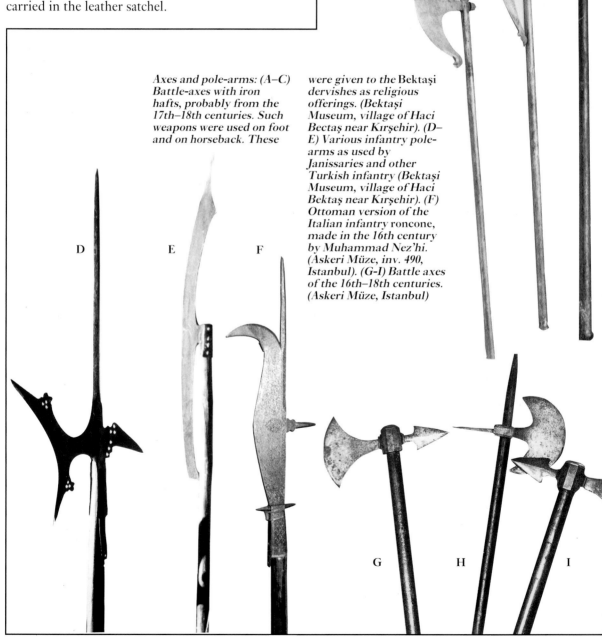

Axes and pole-arms: (A–C) Battle-axes with iron hafts, probably from the 17th–18th centuries. Such weapons were used on foot and on horseback. These were given to the Bektaşi dervishes as religious offerings. (Bektaşi Museum, village of Haci Bectaş near Kırşehir). (D–E) Various infantry pole-arms as used by Janissaries and other Turkish infantry (Bektaşi Museum, village of Haci Bektaş near Kırşehir). (F) Ottoman version of the Italian infantry roncone, made in the 16th century by Muhammad Nez'hi. (Askeri Müze, inv. 490, Istanbul). (G-I) Battle axes of the 16th–18th centuries. (Askeri Müze, Istanbul)

H2: Bektaşi dervish

If the spiritual support offered by orthodox *Imams* was too intellectual for ordinary soldiers, they could turn to *Bektaşi* dervishes, who had close links with the Janissary *Ocak*. Their religion was of a much more mystical, sometimes 'homespun' and relaxed type. Compared to the stark and puritanical uniform of the official *Imam*, this *Bektaşi* has almost all the symbolic objects associated with his sect: a vest cut in a woman's style; a buffalo horn on a leather strap; a plaited leather horse-halter around his waist beneath his sash; a rosary of 100 wooden beads; a *teslim taşi* or 'surrender stone' of white alabaster, with 12 grooves and 12 points; a girdle of white wool; and an axe decorated with a *Qur'anic* verse and a religious poem.

H3: Kulluk of the Ellialtı Neferi, patrolman of 56th Orta, 18th century

The Janissary Corps always had a public-order role in Istanbul, but in later years some units operated as little more than a local police force. The *Ellialtı* or 56th *Orta*, for example, were responsible for the 'Produce and Fruit Pier' where fresh food was brought to the capital. Though he still has a *Yatağan* sword, this man's heavy truncheon was probably more useful for such duties.

Plate I: Mehter military band

I1: Mehterbaşı Ağa conductor

The uniforms of the *Mehterhane* military band differed from those of European military bands in one important feature: whereas Western armies made their bandsmen look magnificent, the Turks did the opposite, giving musicians plain uniforms. Even the conductor shown here has a coat of simple shape though of magnificent fabric). His *Külâh* hat is red, like that of leaders of instrumental sections. The *çevgân* with which he keeps time is a more elaborate version of that used by some NCOs. Larger *çevgâns* would later be adopted by various central European armies, where they were known as 'jingling Johnnies'.

'Wrestlers'; Ottoman miniatures album, c.1650–85. Apart from being a military exercise, wrestling was the most popular spectator sport in the Ottoman Empire. It was watched by both men and women, though the two groups were kept strictly separated. This picture also shows the typical Ottoman haircut, in which the entire head was shaved except for a small tuft on top. (Private collection)

'Weapons bazaar in Istanbul'; Ottoman miniatures album, c. 1650–85. Such albums showing Ottoman life and costume were made for European visitors. Their artistic quality is low but they include interesting and humorous details rarely found in more serious Ottoman miniature painting. This shop sells swords, daggers, archery equipment, maces and clothes. (Private collection)

I2: Zurnazen clarinet player

Of all the instruments used by the *Mehterhane*, the *zurna* or oriental clarinet gave the most distinctive sound. It was made of plum or apricot wood and was basically the same as a medieval European *chalumeau*. The *Zurnazen* himself wears a plain *cübbe* coat, baggy *şalvar* trousers, a broad *şal* cummerbund and the blue hat of an ordinary musician.

I3: Mehter Ağası of Köszen, leader of kettle-drum section

As an *Ağa* or leader of a musical section, this kettle-drummer has a red hat. The only other distinctive features are the riding boots, worn because he is a member of a mounted band. *Kös* (massive kettle-

Interior of a large and highly decorated late 17th century Ottoman tent as used by senior commanders on campaign. (Askeri Müze, Istanbul). Detail of the Janissary lantern hanging in the tent. Its paper covering is painted with the emblem of the 4th Orta of the Bostancı Bölük. (Askeri Müze, Istanbul)

drums) had been used to inspire Islamic armies and terrify their enemies for a thousand years, and it was common for them to be mounted on camels so that they could accompany an army into battle.

Plate J: Support personnel
Plate J1: Aşçı cook

To describe an *Aşçı* or 'cook' as support personnel could be misleading as the term referred to a Janissary junior officer or NCO. It was, however, rooted in the Janissary *Ocak*'s early history. On parade the *Aşçıs* carried an *Orta*'s most prized symbol – its *Kazan* or great cooking pot. The uniform of this *Aşçı* suggests that he dates from the 18th century. His short jacket is of the *mintan* type, worn over a *yelek* waistcoat tucked into exceptionally baggy trousers, the lower parts of which are secured by fabric garters.

J2: Orta Sakası battalion water-carrier

Several illustrations show *Saka* water-carriers wearing thick leather jackets that are shorter than those worn by an *Usta*. The almost 'winged' leather collar may have served as shoulder pads for carrying heavy weights such as a large leather water-bottle. The

object resembling a camel-whip might have kept thirsty soldiers at bay. This man also has the symbol and number of the 15th *Cemaat Orta* tattooed on his arm.

J3: Bostancı Aşçısı 'cook', junior officer of a Bostancı battalion

One detail of this uniform that distinguished the *Bostancı* division was a bag-like red *Barata* cap though this was also worn by some Palace servants. The fact that a *Bostancı Aşçısı* was sometimes shown with a cloth over his shoulder and several bags in his hand suggests that he was still involved in cooking the unit's meal, if only in a supervisory role.

J4: Woman from Mitilini, 16th century

The female costume of areas such as the Aegean islands retained several pre-Ottoman features. The overall cut of this woman's dress recalls that of Renaissance Italy, but the peak on her hat, designed to avoid a peasant-like tan, was adopted by upper class ladies in many parts of the Ottoman Empire.

Plate K: The Bostancı Corps
Plate K1: Bostancı Binbaşı, 18th century

The basic *Bostancı* uniform was red, the *Binbaşı*'s status being shown by the fullness of his coat, its long sleeves and the thickly embroidered, gold 'frogging'

The Qala'at al Hasa fort, built in 1757–74 to protect the strategic military road across the Jordanian desert from Damascus to Aqaba on the Red Sea. Like earlier Ottoman fortifications, it was strictly functional. The entrance to the Qala'at al Hasa was, however, decorated with a series of simple pictures of ships in a style similar to those on early medieval Egyptian paper 'good luck charms'. (author's photograph)

down the front. The large trench-mortar that these officers are studying was among several extraordinary weapons used successfully by Ottoman infantry in siege warfare. It threw grenades, and was cocked and then fired by pulling two separate cords.

K2: Bostancı Nefer soldier of the 3rd rank, 17th century

This *Bostancı Nefer* or ordinary soldier may have the clothes a soldier wore when working, rather than when on parade or in active service. He has removed his tall padded *barata* hat but retains his *takke* skull-cap. The shoulders of his sleeveless front-opening *tennure* have black horse-hair tassels, the significance of which is unknown. The outer yellow sash shows him to be a soldier of the 3rd grade, while the tattoo on his arm is that of the 8th *Bölük Orta*, perhaps originally a naval or harbour-guard unit.

K3: Bostancı Kethüdası officer

This *Kethüda*, a senior battalion officer of a *Bostancı Bölük*, has a *Külâh* hat and turban similar to that worn by the *Mehterhane* band. The double-breasted wrap-over *kaftan* beneath his coat is old-fashioned, and the broad-sleeved *cübbe* worn over it is also very traditional. His yellow boots show him to belong to

'Punishing a man found drunk in public'; Ottoman miniatures album, c.1650–75. Janissary units included men and officers specifically responsible for punishing offenders. One of the most common forms of punishment was the falaka, a supple wand used to beat the soles of a convicted man's feet. (Private collection)

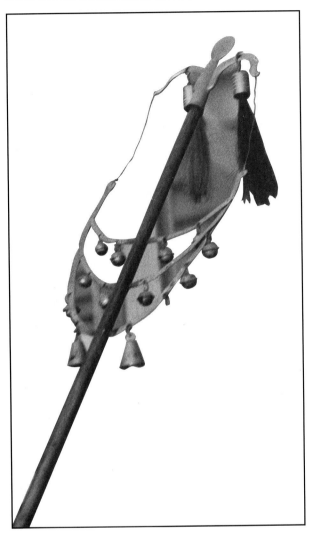

scripts. The most obvious was an extraordinary form of cap on which the brim is cut into four flaps. These were also worn by artillerymen and people of Balkan origin, though having the two front flaps tied up behind a turban is associated with infantry soldiers. Otherwise, this individual's clothes are typical of the Balkan provinces of the Ottoman Empire, while his musket and *tırpan* glaive are specifically Turkish.

L2: Azap, 16th–17th centuries
The *Azaps* did have a uniform, though less is known about it than about Janissary dress. They wore small, tightly wound turbans and the same type of *dolama* coat as the Janissaries. Some manuscripts suggest that *Azaps* wore green coats, so there was probably variation in colour. Once again, this soldier's weaponry reflects the military influences felt in the Ottoman Empire: his *teber* axe is similar to those used in western Mediterranean countries; his shield is distinctly Balkan or eastern European; while his *şaşka* or guardless sabre comes from the Caucasus.

L3: Sekbanbaşı officer of the Sekban corps
This battalion officer of the *Sekban* corps wears another type of thick leather coat with wing-like collars. It too is decorated with metallic additions. The fearsome *kamçı* whip thrust into his belt may have been used to control undisciplined troops, but is more likely to have been a symbolic relic from the days when *Sekbans* really were 'keepers of the Sultan's hunting dogs', and as such would be a mark of office.

An Ottoman officer's çevgen, a staff with horsehair tassels and a series of small bells. It was used to keep time during a recruit's early training and by the singers in an Ottoman Mehterhane or military band. (Askeri Müze, Istanbul)

an elite unit. The sabre's scabbard has three suspension rings, enabling it to be hung vertically while on foot or at an angle while riding. The flintlock musket is of a distinctly Turkish form, developed from an earlier matchlock arquebus of similar shape.

Plate L: Other infantry forces
Plate L1: Levent, late 16th century
The precise uniform of the *Levent* corps has not been identified – perhaps the corps never had one. On the other hand, certain features do seem to have been associated with *Levents* in various Ottoman manu-

Bibliography
F. Babingen, *Mehmet the Conqueror and his Time* (Princeton 1978).

K.K. Barbir, *Ottoman Rule in Damascus 1708–1758* (Princeton 1980).

J.K. Birge, *The Bektashi Order of Dervishes* (London 1965).

F. Bodur, *Türk Maden Sanatı: The Art of Turkish Metalworking* (Istanbul 1987).

A. Cevat (trans. G. Macrides), *Etat Militaire Ottoman*, vol. I, book 1 in *Les Corps des Janissaires* (Constantinople 1882).

A. Clot, *Suleiman the Magnificent: The Man, His Life, His Epoch* (London 1992).

The two main Janissary barracks in Istanbul were demolished in the 19th century, but this building, the Tophane or artillery store, overlooking the Bosphorus, survives. Its barracks were added by Bayazit II in the late 15th or early 16th century and were probably similar to Janissary barracks. (Author's photograph)

J. Deny, *Chansons de janissaires turcs d'Alger* (Brussels 1925).

J. Deny, 'Les registres de solde des Janissaires . . . d'Alger', *Revue Africaine*, LXI (1920).

S. Doras & Ş. Kocaman, *Osmanlılar Albümü* (illustrated history of Ottoman uniforms and military organisation) (Istanbul 1983).

Encyclopedia of Islam, 1st edit., 'Janissaries'.

Encyclopedia of Islam, 2nd edit., 'Barud: Ottomans', 'Devshirme', 'Ghulam: Ottoman Empire', 'Harb: Ottomans'.

H.A.R. Gibb & H. Bowen, *Islamic Society and the West*. vol. I: *Islamic Society in the Eighteenth Century* (two parts) (London 1950 & 1957).

G. Goodwin, *The Janissaries* (London 1994).

M.L. Gross, 'The origins and role of the Janissaries

Archery practice in the Ok Meydan'; Ottoman miniatures album, c. 1650–5. Soldiers and civilians practised archery as a sport as well as a military exercise. The numerous pillars served as range markers. Two men are also reading the inscription on a pillar that probably commemorates a notable long-distance shot. (Private collection)

in early Ottoman history', *Middle East Research Association* (1969–70).

H. Inalcik, *The Ottoman Empire: The Classical Age 1300–1600* (London 1973).

G. Kaldy-Nagy, 'The Holy War (jihad) in the first centuries of the Ottoman Empire', *Harvard Ukrainian Studies*, III–IV (1979–80).

P.E. Klopsteg, *Turkish Archery and the Composite Bow* (Evanston 1947).

R.E. Koçu, *Yeniçeriler* (popular history of the Janissaries, in Turkish) (Istanbul 1964).

F. Kurtoğlu, *Türk Bayrağı ve ayyıldiz* (history of Turkish flags and emblems) (Ankara 1938).

L.F. Marsigli, *L'Etat Militaire de l'Empire Ottoman* (The Hague 1732).

B. Miller, *The Palace School of Mohammed the Conqueror* (Cambridge, Mass. 1941).

A. North, *Islamic Arms* (London 1985).

A. Pallis, *In the Days of the Janissaries: Old Turkish Life as depicted in the 'Travel Book' of Evliyá Chelebí* (London 1951).

J.A.B. Palmer, 'The Origins of the Janissaries', *Bulletin of the John Rylands Library*, XXXV (1952–53).

V.J. Parry & M.E. Yapp (edit.), *War, Technology and Society in the Middle East* (London 1975). Articles by: H. Inalcik, *'The Socio-political effects of the diffusion of fire-arms in the Middle East'*; V.J. Parry *'La Manière de combattre'*; A.K. Rafeq, *'The local forces in Syria in the seventeenth and eighteenth centuries'*.